Easy to Read Bible Summary for Teens and Adults

Michael Kotch

WESTBOW
P R E S S®
A DIVISION OF THOMAS NELSON
& ZONDERVAN

WestBow Press books may be ordered through booksellers or by contacting:

WestBow Press
A Division of Thomas Nelson & Zondervan
1663 Liberty Drive
Bloomington, IN 47403
www.westbowpress.com
1 (866) 928-1240

ISBN: 978-1-9736-4767-6 (sc)
ISBN: 978-1-9736-4766-9 (hc)
ISBN: 978-1-9736-4768-3 (e)

Library of Congress Control Number: 2018914412

Print information available on the last page.

WestBow Press rev. date: 12/10/2018

Contents

Preface

This Bible summary covers all of the major stories and themes of the Bible from the first words in the Book of Genesis, to the last words in the Book of revelation. It is written in clear and simple language that is easy to understand. It is intended for a person who always wanted to get a general understanding of the entire Bible, but for whatever reason, never read all of it. This book is also ideal for teens to learn all about the Bible on their own, or for parents to use to teach the Bible to their children.

Interwoven through the book is an explanation of how all of the Bible connects together and points to Jesus Christ. The Old Testament is the fall of man as well as man's attempts to follow God by following his laws. Mankind tried to do it but was too weak and kept on sinning. I explain through the connected stories in the Old Testament why we needed a Savior. This Savior, Jesus, arrived in the New Testament with a salvation plan for all of us that would work.

Please understand that this book is not a replacement for reading the Bible. The Bible is actually the word of God. Everyone should read it, and read it regularly. This book is a summary of the Bible. It is an excellent way to get an overview of the Bible, to use as a Biblical reference, and to introduce the Bible to Teens and children who may not yet be able to yet read the entire Bible on their own.

Chapter 1

Introduction and Overview

Brief Summary of the Bible, God's Plans for Us, and Why Jesus Is Important

God is our Father. One of the ways he chooses to talk with us, his children, is to send personal messages about him to us. This is the Bible. In the Bible, God explains who he is, who we are as his children, what things he wants us to do, and which things he will do for us. In this first chapter, I will give you an overview of what the Bible is about and why we need to read it.

God created human beings because he wanted a family to love and be with. He created man and woman as sinless. God would appear to the first man and woman (Adam and Eve) and be with them in person. The Bible talks about God walking with Adam and Eve in the cool of the evening in the garden of Eden. They were without sin, and they had a close relationship with God.

God wants all human beings to go to heaven and be with him when they die. However, heaven is a sinless place. Heaven is where God lives, and sin is not allowed there. If a person committed a sin, he or she is not allowed in. God gave man and woman free will. (They could choose whether or not they wanted to listen to God.) God did not want them to be like robots or slaves who could not choose what they wanted to do.

When God was with Adam and Eve in the garden of Eden, he told them that they were not allowed to eat fruit from the Tree of the Knowledge of Good and Evil. The devil talked Adam and Eve into going against what God told them, and they ate from the tree. This was a sin, and because of this, when they died, they would not be allowed into heaven because heaven does not allow sin to enter into it.

Sin was like a virus that infected their souls and was passed on to the souls of all of their children. For example, Adam and Eve's first children were Cain and Abel. Cain got mad at Abel over a small matter, and he killed him. Sin was already horribly affecting humankind right from the start with Adam and Eve and their children, Cain and Abel. There was no hope for humankind to get to heaven without God's help.

God loves people, and he wants all of us to love and follow him while we are on the earth before being with him in heaven as his children when we die. Therefore, God gave us his first plan to save us from sin so we could get to heaven. He gave us the law. The Old Testament in the Bible is filled with laws, or rules. If we follow these perfectly, we will not commit any sins, and we will get to heaven. One of the examples of these laws is the Ten Commandments.

There were many laws and rules in the Old Testament of the Bible. (The Old Testament is about the time before Jesus came; the New Testament starts when Jesus came to the earth, and it is all about him.) Humankind tried to follow these rules, but people were weak and kept messing up and breaking the rules. (They kept sinning.)

The Old Testament focuses on the nation of Israel. God said that he made all of the nations of the world, yet he wanted a nation that would be his own special one. He chose Israel to be this nation just because he wanted to—not because they were better than anyone else was. He also chose Israel as his own personal nation because of a promise he made to Abraham, who was willing to make a very big sacrifice to God because God asked him to. We will read about this soon.

The Old Testament is the story of the people of Israel trying to follow God's laws and rules. They would be in a lot of trouble as a result of the sins they committed. They would cry out to God for help, and he would save them. They would be good for a while but start to mess up and sin again. Their sins would get worse and worse until really bad things would eventually happen to them. They would cry out to God, and he would save them again. And then they would start to sin, their sins would get really bad, and so on.

This pattern happened over and over again throughout the Old Testament. God's first plan was perfect: if the people followed his laws and rules, they would not sin. The problem was the people were too weak and sinful to follow it.

God came up with a second plan to save us from our sins so we could be friends with him while we are on the earth and go to heaven to be with him when we die. God the Father, God the Son (Jesus), and God the Holy Spirit decided that Jesus would come to the earth and become a human like all of us, while still remaining fully God. All of the sins that people committed in their lifetimes (including us) would be taken off us and placed on Jesus. He would be punished in our place by being crucified and put to death as punishment for the sins that everyone in the world committed. Whoever accepts Jesus as his or her God and accepts his sacrifice of being punished in our place for the sins we committed now has no sins in the eyes of God.

Jesus was punished in our place with our sins placed on him, so now God now declares us innocent of sin. By accepting Jesus and what he did for us, we can go to heaven when we die. If we do not accept Jesus and what he did for us, then our sins return to us. We would be rejecting the plan God made for us to make us sinless. God would then declare us guilty of our sins when we die. We now could not get into heaven because sin is not allowed there. Instead we would go to a place where people who reject Jesus and what he did for us go—hell.

The Old Testament shows why we need a Savior. (We are too weak to follow God's laws that were designed to prevent us from sinning.) The New Testament is about the Savior (Jesus). He came and took all of our sins on himself, and he was put to death with our sins on him. Now God can declare us innocent of sin so we can be friends with him while we are on the earth and go to heaven when we die.

Chapter 2

The Bible

The Bible is divided into two sections. The first section is the Old Testament. This is before Jesus was born. In the Old Testament, God gave people rules that he wanted them to follow so they could be good and go to heaven when they died. People tried to follow these rules, but they kept messing up (sinning) because people were weak. When the people sinned, God would punish them. God gave us a much easier plan to follow in the New Testament.

The New Testament is when Jesus was born. In the New Testament, God (Jesus) became a man and came to the earth. He took all of our sins on himself and was punished in our place so we don't have to be punished for our sins. All we have to do is accept what he did for us and listen to him. If we do this, God will be happy with us. We will now start at the beginning of the Bible. This is the book of Genesis, the first book of the Bible in the Old Testament.

The Book of Genesis

Before the Flood

The Bible starts with the Old Testament, which is before Jesus came to earth to save us. The first book of the Bible is Genesis. In the beginning, there was God and the angels that lived with him in heaven. However, he did not make the universe in which we live in yet. At one point, he decided he wanted to make our universe and make us to live in it on the earth. He made the universe in six God days. We do not know how long a God day is.

On the first day, the universe did not exist yet, and everything outside of heaven was dark. Then God said, "Let there be light." God's light then filled everything.

On the second day, God made a separation between heaven and the universe. Then God made the earth, and he separated the oceans from the dry land. On the third day, God made all the plants, trees, flowers, fruits, and vegetables on the earth. On the fourth day, God made the sun to light the day as well as the moon and stars to light the night. Before the sun and the moon, it was the light from God that lit up everything.

On the fifth day, God made all of the birds in the sky and all of the fish and sea creatures. On the sixth day, God made all of the rest of the animals on the earth.

Also on the sixth day, God decided to make man in his own image. The first man that God made was named Adam. The first woman that God made was named Eve. God told them that they would be in charge of everything alive on the earth. The place on the earth where Adam and Eve lived was called the garden of Eden.

After God made man and woman, his work of creating everything in the universe and on earth was finished, so God rested on the seventh day.

Adam and Eve's Sin Against God (The Fall)

God placed Adam and Eve as rulers over all of the animals on earth. God allowed Adam to name all of the animals that existed. God would walk and talk with Adam and Eve in the garden of Eden. There were all kinds of plants, fruit, and vegetables in the garden of Eden for Adam and Eve to eat. In the middle of the garden of Eden was the Tree of the Knowledge of Good and Evil.

God said to Adam and Eve, "You may surely eat of every tree of the garden, but of the tree of the knowledge of good and evil you shall not eat, for in the day that you eat it, you shall surely die" (Genesis 2:16–17).

One day, the devil, an enemy of God, came to Eve disguised as a serpent. He decided to lie to Adam and Eve to mess up their relationship with God because he is evil. He said to Eve, "Did God tell you not to eat from the Tree of Knowledge of Good and Evil or said you would die? You will not die! God is lying to you. He does not want you to eat from it because, if you do, you will become powerful like him."

Eve went against what God told her, and she ate from the tree. She then gave fruit from this tree to Adam, and he ate from it too. Adam and Eve immediately knew they were wrong in doing what God said not to do. God appeared and confronted Adam and Eve. Because Adam and Eve sinned against God, God told them that they had to leave the garden of Eden.

Their lives and the lives of all of their children (us) would not be easy like it was before they sinned against God. They would now have to work hard to survive. Also they would get old and die one day, as God warned them they would if they ate of the fruit of the Tree of Knowledge of Good and Evil. Because of their sin, they would not be able to get into heaven when they died unless God decided to help them because heaven is a sinless place. God still cared for them, however. He made them clothes, and he looked out for them.

Cain and Abel

Adam and Eve were husband and wife, and they had a son and named him Cain. They then had a second son and named him Abel. Cain became a farmer; Abel became a shepherd of sheep. Since God loved them and took care of them, Cain and Abel brought presents to God. Abel brought his best sheep as a present to God. Cain, however, kept the best food that he grew for himself and brought God unacceptable food as a gift.

God liked Abel's gift, but he did not like Cain's. Cain became very angry about this. God said to Cain, "Why are you angry? If you bring me good gifts like your brother does, I will be happy with them." Cain became jealous of his brother and killed Abel. This was the first murder in history.

God said to Cain, "What did you do? You killed your brother! Because of this, you will be cursed and will wander around the earth." God still loved Cain even though he killed his brother, and he watched over Cain so that nothing bad would happen to him. God made a wife for Cain, and they had children. Adam and Eve, Cain's parents, also had more children. Back then, God allowed people to live to be over nine hundred years old. People kept having children, and over time, the earth was full of people.

Noah and the Ark

People multiplied greatly on the earth. Over time, the people became increasingly evil. God shortened their lives to a maximum of 120 years because of this. (There is nobody alive today over 120 years old.) People continued to get progressively evil, however. They got so bad that God became sorry that he made people.

God decided that he would destroy everything alive—people, animals, and plants—on earth with a flood because the entire world was so evil. However, a man named Noah was good. God decided he would save him from the flood and repopulate the earth from his offspring.

God told Noah to make a boat called an ark. He told Noah to put his family in the ark, along with one male and one female of every animal on earth, and to bring food to feed everyone and every animal. It took Noah several decades to build the ark, but one day it was finally finished. God sent all of the animals to Noah to put on the ark, and Noah and his family got in. God sealed the door so the water would not get in.

God then sent rain to the earth for forty days and forty nights, and the world was flooded. He also caused water to spring up from inside the earth. The water was so high that it covered all of the mountains on the earth. All of the people in the world drowned because they were so evil, but God saved Noah and his family.

Noah and his family floated in the ark for 150 days. Finally the flood started to go away. The ark landed on the top of a mountain called Mount Ararat. Noah, his family, and all of the animals finally got out of the ark. God made a promise to Noah that he would never again send a worldwide flood. He sent a rainbow to Noah and told him that, every time we see a rainbow, it is God remembering that he will never again wipe out mankind with a flood.

The Tower of Babel

After Noah's family came out of the ark, they had children, grandchildren, and great-grandchildren and became many people. God told them to spread out and fill the earth with people. They did not listen to God. Instead they grouped into one city and built a great tower that went way up into the sky.

Everybody at this time spoke the same language. To force the people to spread out over the earth, like he wanted them to, God confused everyone's language so people could not understand each other. When they tried to speak with each other, it sounded like they were babbling. This caused them to call the tower that they built the Tower of Babel. It also caused the people to spread out from each other and fill the earth, like God wanted them to.

Chapter 3

God Starts the Jewish/Christian Religion with Abraham

After the fall of the Tower of Babel, people spread out over the earth and multiplied. There was a man named Abram. God came to Abram and told him, if you do the things I tell you to do, I will bless you and make you a great nation. Your children, grandchildren, and great-grandchildren will be as numerous as the sand grains on the seashore. God then changed Abram's name to Abraham after he made this promise with him.

At this time, two cities, Sodom and Gomorrah, did very evil things. God told Abraham that he would destroy these two cities because they were so evil. This made Abraham sad. He asked God, "If you could find just ten people who were not evil in these cities, would you not destroy them?"

God said that he would not destroy the cities if he could find ten good people in them. God looked as hard as he could, but he could not find ten people who were not evil. So he had to destroy the cities. God allowed Abraham to save his nephew Lot and his family from Sodom before he destroyed it.

Before God destroyed Sodom and Gomorrah, he sent down two angels to the cities to meet the people who lived there to make sure that they were evil. When the two angels arrived, the people were so evil that they tried to beat up and kill the angels.

God had seen enough. He rained fire and brimstone down on Sodom and Gomorrah, completely destroying both cities.

Abraham Failed God's First Test

When God first appeared to Abraham, he told him that he would give Abraham and his wife, Sarah, children. Abraham and Sarah were now old, and they did not have any children yet. They thought that God had broken his promise with them. God never breaks promises that he makes. He waited to see if they would trust him that he would keep his promise.

Abraham and Sarah thought that God did not come through on his promise that they would have children since they were around ninety years old at this time. Sarah told Abraham that he should have a child with her servant named Hagar since God had failed in his promise to give them children.

Abraham had a son with Hagar and named him Ishmael. God appeared to Abraham and told him again that he would give him children with Sarah. Next year, Sarah had Abraham's son, and they named him Isaac. Abraham was one hundred years old; Sarah was ninety years old.

Both Sarah and Abraham learned that they needed to trust what God tells them. Nothing is impossible with God, and he always keeps his end of a promise with us, as long as we keep ours.

God Puts Abraham to a Second Test to See If Abraham Will Trust and Follow God

Abraham's son, Isaac, grew into a nice boy, and Abraham and Sarah loved Isaac very much. God put Abraham to a very difficult test to see if Abraham would follow God's instructions. God told Abraham to take Isaac into the wilderness, and once they were there, he was to tie up Isaac and offer him as a sacrifice to God.

Abraham was extremely sad about this. But he listened to God and trusted him that somehow God would make everything ok. He took Isaac, whom he loved very much, on a trip into the wilderness. When they got there, Abraham tied up Isaac and pulled out a knife to kill him, like God had told him to.

As Abraham lifted up his knife to kill Isaac, God immediately went to Abraham and said "Abraham, Abraham!"

And Abraham said, "Here am I."

God said, "Do not lay your hand on the boy or do anything to him, for now I know that you fear God, seeing that you have not withheld your son, your only son, from me. By myself I have sworn, declares the Lord, because you have done this and have not withheld your son, your only son, I will surely bless you, and I will surely multiply your children and grandchildren as the stars of heaven and as the sand that is on the seashore. And in your children and grandchildren shall all of the nations of the earth be blessed because you have obeyed my voice" (Genesis 22:11–18).

Because Abraham trusted God and tried to do what God told him to do, God made it so that his children and grandchildren would found the country of Israel. Additionally, one of Abraham's great-great-grandchildren would be Jesus, who would save the world from their sins.

Isaac Has a Son Named Jacob

Isaac grew into a man who had a son named Jacob. Jacob tricked his twin brother, Esau, out of his firstborn birthright blessing. Esau wanted to kill Jacob because of this. Jacob was afraid that Esau would in fact kill him, so he moved far away.

God came to Jacob in a dream and told him that he had made a promise to his grandfather, Abraham, that his descendants would be many and would form a great nation, starting with Jacob's sons.

Jacob got married, and he and his wife had twelve sons, who would go on to form twelve tribes, which would later become the country of Israel.

Israel is the country in which Jesus would later be born in when he came to earth from heaven.

God came to Jacob one night, and Jacob asked God to bless him. God hesitated to bless Jacob, so Jacob began to wrestle with God to try to get God to bless him. Jacob and God wrestled all night long.

When God saw that Jacob would not give up, he touched Jacob's hip socket and caused it to pop out of joint. This caused Jacob to limp for the rest of his life to remind him of the day he wrestled with God.

Jacob still would not stop wrestling with God until God blessed him. God asked Jacob his name, and he said "Jacob."

Then God said to Jacob, "Your name shall no longer be called Jacob, but your new name will be Israel, for you have wrestled with God and men and have prevailed" (Genesis 32:27–28). This is where the country of Israel began. Jacob became the first person to form Israel, and his twelve sons would go on to form the twelve tribes that would make up Israel. God then finally blessed Jacob as he asked him to.

Chapter 4

God Uses Joseph's Difficult Trials for Good

Jacob had twelve sons: Reuben, Simeon, Levi, Judah, Issachar, Zebulun, Joseph, Benjamin, Dan, Naphtali, Gad, and Asher. Joseph was the second-youngest son of Jacob. Jacob loved Joseph the most out of all of his sons, which bothered his older brothers.

Jacob made Joseph a robe of many colors, which Joseph wore. When his brothers saw this, they became jealous and hated Joseph. Joseph was seventeen years old, and he had two dreams. He told his brothers the first dream.

Joseph said, "Behold, we were binding sheaves of wheat in the field, and my sheaf arose and stood upright. And behold, your sheaves gathered around it and bowed down to my sheaf."

His brothers said, "Are you indeed to reign and rule over us?"

His second dream was "Behold, the sun, the moon, and eleven stars were bowing down to me" (Genesis 37:6–9).

Both his father and his brothers criticized Joseph for these dreams he had.

One day, Joseph's older brothers were watching a flock of sheep in a field far away. Jacob sent Joseph to them to see if they needed his help. His brothers saw Joseph coming from far away. They were jealous of him and plotted to kill him. His oldest brother, Reuben, said it would be very wrong to kill their brother. He said they should put him in a pit until they figured out what to do with him.

They grabbed him, took off his robe of many colors, and put him in a pit. While Reuben was away working, a bunch of slave traders passed by. His other brothers decided to sell Joseph to the slave traders for twenty pieces of silver. They took Joseph's robe, ripped it up, and put animal blood on it. They went home and told Jacob that a fierce wild animal had killed Joseph. Jacob was heartbroken over this for many years because he loved Joseph very much.

Joseph was taken to Egypt as a slave. A man named Potiphar, who was captain of Pharaoh's guard, bought him. God was with Joseph and blessed everything that he did. As a result, Joseph was successful at everything he did in his service to Potiphar.

Potiphar noticed that Joseph was successful at everything he did, so he made Joseph overseer of his house and put him in charge of all that he had.

Joseph was a handsome man, and Potiphar's wife was attracted to him. Day after day, she would ask Joseph to lay with her. Joseph would not do it because he knew it was wrong to lay with another man's wife.

One day when no one was in the house except for Joseph and Potiphar's wife, she grabbed him by his shirt and yelled, "Lay with me!" He refused because it was wrong. She would not let him go, so he pulled away, and it ripped his shirt off.

She got angry because Joseph rejected her. She had his shirt in her hand. She lied to the guards and said that Joseph had tried to force himself on her. She had ripped his shirt off as she tried to get away. She also told her husband this lie when he got home from work. He had Joseph arrested and put in prison.

However, God was with Joseph and blessed everything he did in prison so it would be successful. As a result, Joseph was put in charge of all of the prisoners in the prison.

While Joseph was in prison, Pharaoh's cupbearer and baker were accused of stealing from Pharaoh, and they were put in prison with Joseph. Both of them had a dream while they were sleeping and were troubled by it because they did not know what it meant. They told their dreams to Joseph, and God told Joseph the meanings of their visions.

God told Joseph that the cupbearer's dream meant that in three days he would be declared innocent of his crime and be released from prison. The baker's dream meant that in three days he would be found guilty of his crime and be put to death for it.

That is exactly what happened. The cupbearer was very happy that he was released from prison. He promised Joseph that he would help him get out of prison for interpreting his dream, but once released, he forgot about Joseph. Joseph remained in prison for two more years.

Two years later, Pharaoh had two troublesome dreams. In the first dream, seven healthy cows walked out of the Nile River. Shortly after that, seven skinny and sickly cows walked out of the Nile River and ate the healthy cows. In the second dream, seven plump and healthy ears of corn grew out of the ground. Right after that, seven skinny and dried-up ears of corn grew and ate up the healthy ears of corn. When Pharaoh woke up, he was very upset about these dreams. He asked all of the wise men of Egypt if they could tell him what these dreams meant, but no one could.

Then the chief cupbearer remembered that Joseph had interpreted his dream two years ago when he was in prison. He told Pharaoh that Joseph might be able to interpret his dreams. Pharaoh sent for Joseph and told Joseph his two dreams.

Joseph said that God would interpret the dreams and tell him what they meant. Joseph said that the dream about the healthy and sickly cows and corn meant the same thing. There would be seven years of great crops, followed by seven years of severe famine in which the crops would not grow and there would be no food. He told Pharaoh that, during the seven years of good crops, he needed to take one-fifth of the crops and store them up to be used during the seven years of famine after that so they would have food during the famine.

Pharaoh was extremely pleased that God had told Joseph what his dreams meant. He said that, because God was clearly with Joseph in everything he did, he made Joseph second-in- command over all of Egypt behind him, and everyone in Egypt had to do whatever Joseph said.

Joseph was thirty years old when he was made second-in-command over Egypt. Pharaoh's dreams came true, just as God told Joseph they would. There was seven years of plenty during which the Egyptians saved up one fifth of their crops each year in storehouses. After this came seven years of famine in which crops would not grow.

Joseph opened up the storehouses and sold this food not only to the Egyptians but also to neighboring countries hit by the famine. The famine also hit Joseph's father, Jacob (Israel), and his eleven brothers, who had sold him to the slave traders thirteen years ago.

Jacob (Israel) instructed his eleven sons to go to Egypt to buy food because they had none due to the famine. When the eleven brothers got there, they had to go to Joseph because he was in charge of handing out all of the food. Joseph recognized his brothers and had his guards take them to the prison, accusing them of being spies.

They did not recognize Joseph, and they were very afraid. Joseph asked them if they had any other brothers. They confessed and said they had another brother, Joseph, whom they had sold into slavery thirteen years ago because they were very jealous of him. They were sorry for doing this, and they started to cry and say they deserved whatever punishment they got now for doing this to Joseph.

Joseph said to them, "Take a good look at my face. I am your brother, Joseph, whom you sold into slavery. I am now second-in-command of all of Egypt, and I have the power to do whatever I want with you."

Joseph's brothers began to panic. They were sure that Joseph would have them killed for selling him into slavery. He acted like he was very mad at them. What do you think Joseph did to his brothers? He did not punish them.

He said, "God allowed everything to happen the way it did so I could save people's lives. Although you sold me to the slave traders and meant it for bad, God meant it for good. He made everything I did be successful, and it eventually put me second-in-charge of Egypt, where I saved up food to survive the famine. I love you, brothers, and do not be afraid of me."

The brothers were overjoyed that Joseph was alive and doing well. Joseph sent for his father, Jacob. Jacob (Israel) and his eleven sons moved to Egypt and lived with Joseph for the rest of their lives.

Chapter 5

Moses and the Israelites

The Book of Exodus

As time passed, Jacob's (Israel's) twelve sons had children, grandchildren, great-grandchildren, and so on. Many other Israelite people moved to Egypt during the famine. Because of Joseph's wise plan given to him by God on what to do during the famine, Egypt was the only country in the area that had food.

There became a great many people called the Israelites who were living in Egypt. Over a great deal of time, a new Pharaoh was in charge of Egypt, one who had never heard of Joseph. He became afraid of the large number of Israelites living in Egypt, thinking they might one day turn against him.

Pharaoh instructed the commanders beneath him to turn the Israelites into slaves and to treat them harshly. The Israelites helped build cities for Pharaoh as slaves. The more Pharaoh oppressed the Israelites, however, the more they multiplied. Pharaoh instructed the doctors that delivered babies that, if an Israelite or Hebrew woman gave birth to a boy, they would kill the baby boy, but if it were a girl, they would let the girl live.

Pharaoh did this mean thing to reduce the number of Israelites living in Egypt. The doctors refused to do this, and God blessed the doctors for refusing. Pharaoh then gave an order that every boy born of a Hebrew woman would be thrown into the Nile River to drown.

The Birth of Moses

One day, a Hebrew (Israelite/Jewish) woman gave birth to a boy. She hid him for three months so the authorities would not throw him in the Nile River. As he got bigger, she could no longer hide him well. She put the baby in a basket at the edge of the river, and she hid and watched to see what would happen to him.

Pharaoh's daughter came down to the river to take a bath in it. She found the basket with the baby in it. She realized it was a Jewish baby, but she felt sorry for it and adopted it as her own son. Pharaoh's daughter named the boy Moses, which means "I drew him out of the water."

Moses grew into a man. One day, he saw an Egyptian beating a Hebrew, one of his own people. Moses killed the Egyptian and hid him in the sand. Pharaoh found out about this and wanted to kill Moses. Afraid, Moses ran away to a land called Midian. Moses found a wife there and had a son named Gershom. Moses lived here for forty years.

God Hears Israel's Groaning

The people of Israel groaned for many years because of their slavery to Egypt, and they cried out to God for help. God remembered his promise to Abraham, Isaac, and Jacob that he would make their descendants as numerous as the sand on the seashore, so he decided to help.

God appeared to Moses in the form of a bush that was burning yet never burned up. He told Moses that he would send him to Pharaoh to bring the Israelites out of Egypt and into a land that God was setting aside for them.

Moses was afraid to do this. So God told him that he would strengthen him and give him whatever power he needed to bring the Israelites out of slavery in Egypt and into a new land.

Moses returned to Egypt with his family. Moses went to Pharaoh and told him that God said that he needed to let the Israelites go for three days to worship God in the wilderness. Pharaoh became angry at this. He said, not only would he not let the Israelites go to worship God, he would give the Israelites much harder work to do because they had free time on their hands to go worship.

Moses complained to God and asked him why he told him to tell Pharaoh to let his people go worship, which resulted in Pharaoh punishing the Israelites. God said to Moses that he would now see what he would do to Pharaoh for being mean to the Israelites. He told Moses to tell the Israelites that God would free them from being slaves to the Egyptians. He would give them their own land, and he would be their God.

Moses went with his brother, Aaron, to Pharaoh and said, "God said, 'Let my people go.'"

Pharaoh refused. Moses threw the staff he had in his hand on the ground, and it became a snake. Pharaoh had his magicians do the same thing. Moses' snake ate all of the magicians' snakes. Pharaoh was surprised at this, but he still would not let the Israelites go.

Moses said to Pharaoh that he would come back again and demand in the name of God that Pharaoh let the Israelites go. Each time Pharaoh said no.

God would send a plague on the Egyptians until they could take it no longer and finally let the Israelites go. The first time Pharaoh said no, God had Moses turn the water of the Nile River into blood. All the fish died, and the river stunk. The second time, Pharaoh refused to let the Israelites go. God had Moses send a plague of frogs into Egypt. Frogs got into the people's houses and were everywhere!

The third time Pharaoh said no, God had Moses send a plague of gnats (little flies) all over the Egyptians. The fourth time Pharaoh said no, God had Moses send a plague of flies onto the Egyptians. The fifth time Pharaoh said no, all of the livestock of the Egyptians (cows, horses, camels, and so on) died, but the livestock of the Israelites were ok.

The sixth time Pharaoh said no, God sent a plague of boils and sores on the skin of the Egyptian people. The seventh time Pharaoh said no, God had Moses send huge hail onto Egypt, which killed any person or animal that was outside.

The eighth time Pharaoh said no, God had Moses send a plague of locust (grasshoppers) all over Egypt, but they did not bother the Israelites. The ninth time Pharaoh said no, God had Moses send three days of complete darkness over Egypt so they couldn't see anything, but the Israelites had light in their homes.

The Passover

The final plague was the worst one. God had Moses tell Pharaoh that, if he did not let the Israelites go, God would kill the firstborn child and animal of everyone in Egypt. Pharaoh said he would not let the Israelites go. God told each Israelite family to kill a lamb and paint a stripe of its blood across the doorway of each house. This way, God would know which houses were those of the Israelites, and he would pass over that house and not kill the firstborn person or animal of that house.

At midnight, God killed the firstborn of every family that did not have the lamb's blood over its doorpost, including Pharaoh's first son. The Israelites had lamb's blood over all of their doorposts, so their firstborn children and animals were spared. The Egyptians were so upset that Pharaoh finally told the Israelites that they could leave Egypt.

The Parting of the Red Sea

A few days after the Israelites left Egypt, Pharaoh changed his mind about allowing them to leave. He gathered his army and chased after the Israelites to capture them and once again turn them into slaves of the Egyptians. The Egyptian army surrounded the Israelites on three sides. On the fourth side was the Red Sea.

God told Moses to raise his arms in the air. When he did, the Red Sea parted, and the Israelites crossed over the dry sea floor with huge walls of water on each side. When the Israelites crossed the Red Sea, the Egyptian army began to cross the floor of the Red Sea after them.

When all of the Egyptian army was on the dry sea floor, God told Moses to raise his arms in the air again. When he did, the walls of water of the Red Sea came crashing down on the Egyptian army and drowned the entire army, saving the Israelites. Finally God saved the Israelites from being slaves of the Egyptians, and he moved them out of Egypt after being slaves for 430 years.

Moses and the Israelites were walking around outside of Egypt, waiting for God to show them where he would have them live. They got hungry, so God rained down bread from heaven each day like snowflakes. It was called *manna*, and the people would gather it up each day and eat it. The people also wanted meat to eat, so each evening, God made birds called quail fly down and land in the Israelites' camp for the people to cook and eat. When the people got thirsty, God had Moses strike a rock with a stick that he had in his hand, and water would flow out of the rock for the people to drink.

God Gives Moses and the Israelites the Ten Commandments

One day, God told Moses to climb to the top of Mt. Sinai. There, God wrote the Ten Commandments with his finger on two stone tablets. The Ten Commandments are ten rules that God insists that all of us follow. The Ten Commandments are:

1. I am the Lord your God. You shall have no other gods before me.
2. You shall not make and worship a carved image.
3. You shall not take the name of the Lord your God in vain. (Don't curse.)
4. Remember the Sabbath day (Sunday) and keep it holy.
5. Honor your father and mother, and you will have a long life.
6. You shall not murder
7. You shall not commit adultery.
8. You shall not steal.
9. You shall not bear false witness against your neighbor. (Don't lie.)
10. You shall not covet your neighbor's wife or husband or anything that they own.

God then gave the people a bunch of rules and laws that said what he did and didn't want them to do. He also told the Israelites where he was going to have them settle down and live. God told them to make an ark (a really fancy box) where they would store the stone tablets with the Ten Commandments on them.

The Israelites Rebel against God

Moses was up on Mt. Sinai for several days talking with God and getting the Ten Commandments from him. The people went to Moses' brother, Aaron, and asked, "Why is Moses taking so long? Maybe something bad happened to him. He might not come back. We want you to make us new gods that we can follow."

Aaron told the Israelites to give him any gold they had, which they did. He melted down the gold and made a gold statue of a calf. All the people started to worship the golden calf as a god and said that the golden calf, not God, saved the Israelites from the Egyptians.

Meanwhile, God told Moses on Mt. Sinai what the Israelites were doing. God asked Moses if he wanted God to wipe out all of the Israelites because they were so bad and start over with a new nation from Moses' descendants.

Moses said, "No, don't kill them."

God listened to Moses because God and Moses were friends. Moses came down from the mountain and was furious at the Israelites. Out of anger, he smashed the two stone tablets with the Ten Commandments, and he melted the golden calf that the people made.

Moses made a tent that he would go into and talk with God. When Moses would go into the tent, God would come down in the form of a cloud and then go in the tent and talk with Moses. "Thus, the Lord used to speak with Moses face to face, as a man speaks to his friend" (Exodus 33:11). Moses would then tell the Israelites what God said. God had Moses cut two new stone tablets, and God rewrote the Ten Commandments on those tablets.

The Book of Leviticus

In the book of Leviticus, God gave the Israelite people and priests many laws and rules that he wanted them to follow. (Remember, in the Old Testament, God gave the people many laws and rules to follow so they would be sinless, but they were too weak to follow them.) For example, God gave the rule that, if your brother or sister becomes poor and cannot take care of himself or herself without you, you should take care of him or her and be happy when doing it.

The Book of Numbers

Remember that the nation of Israel started with the twelve sons of Jacob. Over 430 years later, by the time that Moses saved the Israelites from the Egyptians, the people of Israel numbered about 2 million people. God would hover over the tent that Moses set up in the midst of the Israelites. In the day, God hovered over the tent in the form of a cloud. At night, God would hover over the tent in the form of fire.

God told Moses to send twelve men into the land of Canaan to act as spies to see who were living there. It was a test to see if they would trust God. Canaan was the land that God intended to give to the Israelites to live in. Ten of the men said they should not go into Canaan because it was inhabited by giants who would defeat them. They did not trust that God would help them defeat these people, even though they saw God destroy the whole Egyptian army.

Two of the spies said, "Yes, there are giants there, but God can defeat them for us."

The Israelites decided to believe that God could not help them defeat the people who lived in Canaan. They became angry at Moses and God, not remembering that God can save them from anyone that he wanted to because he was all powerful. These were the same people who witnessed God do many miracles against Pharaoh in Egypt.

Because of this, God told them to turn around and not enter the land he promised them because they did not believe that God could help them get the land. Instead God had them wander around the wilderness for forty years until all of the people who did not believe God died off. Their children would be given the land that God promised to them. Some of the Israelites went against what God said and tried to take the land of the Canaanites by force. God was not with them, so they lost the battle.

One day, the Israelites were thirsty, and they complained to Moses about it. God told Moses to strike a rock with his staff once so water would come out of it for the people to drink. Moses was angry with the people for complaining about the water because they grumbled to him about everything.

He yelled at them and then slammed his staff down on the rock, and water came out of it for the people to drink. God told Moses that, because he made it look to the people that God was angry with them when he was not, he would not let Moses enter the land that God was giving to the Israelites. He would be able to see it, but he would die before entering it. God told Moses that an Israelite named Joshua would take over Moses' role as leader of the Israelites when Moses died.

Finally, after forty years in the wilderness, the Israelites entered the land of Canaan. This later became the country of Israel, which God had promised them.

The Book of Deuteronomy

The book of Deuteronomy talked more about Moses and the Israelites while they were in the wilderness before God gave them a land to live in. The book of Deuteronomy also gave the people more rules that God wanted them to live by. God stated that the greatest commandment was "You shall love the Lord your God with all your heart, with all your soul, and with all your might." He told the Israelites that he would bless them if they followed him. He said, "Man does not live by bread alone, but by every word that comes from the mouth of the Lord" (Deuteronomy 8:3).

He reminded the Israelites that he took care of them well when they were in the wilderness before they came into the land that God gave them. He told them that, when they became successful, to remember that it was God who blessed them and allowed them to be successful.

Also God said, "Don't think that you are getting good things because you are great people. You are not; you have all sinned. You are getting good things because I love being kind to those who love me. If you love me, I will take care of you well, give you good things, and give you everything that you need."

God said, "Do not worship other gods because there are no other gods. I am the only one, and the rest are false. It makes me very upset when people do that. If you see people that are poor or are in need of something, you need to help these people and be happy about helping them, and I will bless you for it. You must be honest and truthful when dealing with people. Do not lie about other people."

God gave the Israelites many, many other laws or rules to follow in the book of Deuteronomy. (Remember, in the Old Testament, God's first plan to keep us sinless was to give us rules to follow, but we were too weak to follow them all of the time.)

At the end of the book of Deuteronomy, God took Moses to the top of Mount Nebo. He showed Moses the land that he would now give to the Israelites to live in. Moses saw it, but he was not allowed to go into the land because he disobeyed God with the water from the rock. Moses then died. He was buried, and Joshua took over Moses' position as leader of the Israelites.

The Book of Joshua

After Moses died and went to heaven, Joshua took over as the leader of the Israelites as God instructed. God had Joshua lead the army of Israel to take land from bad people and turn it into the land that they would live in. One of the cities that God wanted the Israelites to take for themselves was called Jericho. A big wall surrounded the city of Jericho.

God told the Israelites to march around the entire city each day for six days, and the priests would blow their horns as they walked around the city. On the seventh day, they would march around it seven times with the priests blowing their horns.

After they stopped marching, the people were told to let out a loud shout, and God would knock down Jericho's wall for them. The Israelites did what God told them to do, the wall fell down, and they captured the city to live in, as God wanted them to.

God led Joshua and the Israelite troops. When they followed God's instructions, they conquered and took over cities to live in through the power of God. When they did not listen to God, they were defeated in battle.

The Israelites conquered land and moved into it. Joshua divided this land among the twelve tribes of Israel, which Jacob's twelve sons founded. When this was accomplished, Israel's leader, Joshua, died at the age of 110 years, and he went to heaven. The country of Israel was finally established to the descendants of Abraham, as God had promised him.

Chapter 6

The Book of Judges

Under Joshua, when the Israelites were conquering land to turn it into the country of Israel in which they would live, God told them to drive out all of the people that they conquered because they were evil.

The Israelites disobeyed God and did not do this. They let some of the conquered people stay in the land and live with them. The Israelites began to follow the evil ways of these people. They stopped following God and started to follow false gods. They were doing many evil things that God told them not to do, and they ignored God when he told them to stop these things.

God therefore became angry with the Israelites. God gave them over to the bad people who they now followed, who then conquered and mistreated them. God was against the Israelites, so everything they did failed, and they were in terrible distress.

The Israelites turned back to God and called out to him in their time of troubles. God felt sorry for them, and he wanted to help them. He raised up judges, which were like supermen, to save the Israelites from the people who conquered them.

The problem was, after each time the judges saved the Israelites, the Israelites began to act evil again very quickly and turned away from God. This caused God to remove his protection from them, and without God's help, other nations conquered them. They would cry out to God, he would save them with a judge, and then they would become bad again. This happened over and over. Here is the story of some of the judges that God raised up to save the Israelites.

Because the Israelites acted evil, God allowed the Mesopotamians to conquer them. The Mesopotamians ruled the Israelites for eight years, and the Israelites cried out to God for help. He raised up a judge named Othniel who went to war with the Mesopotamians, conquered them, and freed the Israelites, who then had peace for forty years.

Othniel then died, and the Israelites once again did what was evil in the sight of the Lord. The Lord allowed three countries to conquer the Israelites for eighteen years. The Israelites complained to God, so he raised a judge named Ehud who led an Israeli army rebellion that conquered these three countries. Now they were free again.

Once again, the Israelites acted evil and were conquered by the Philistines. They cried out to God, who raised up a judge named Shamgar who killed six hundred Philistines with an ox bone and freed Israel.

Once free, the Israelites did not learn their lesson, and they acted evil again. A king named Sisera conquered them for twenty years because of this. God rose up two judges: a woman named Deborah and a man named Barak. These two judges helped the Israelites form a rebellion, and they overthrew King Sisera and were once again free.

For some reason, the Israelites again became bad over time and did things that made God angry. He allowed the Midianites to overpower Israel and rule over them in a cruel way for seven years. The Israelites turned back to God and cried out to him to help them. God heard their cries. He rose up one of the most famous judges named Gideon to save them. Gideon was from the weakest tribe of Israel, and he was the weakest man in his tribe.

God told Gideon that he would be a mighty man of valor and he would defeat the Midianites. Gideon found this hard to believe because he was shy and weak. Gideon asked God if he could put him to two tests, to make sure God was actually telling him to do this. God agreed to let Gideon put him to two tests, and he passed both. Once Gideon was convinced that God was telling him to defeat the Midianites, he agreed to do whatever God told him to do.

Gideon gathered 32,000 soldiers of Israel to fight the Midianites, who had 135,000 soldiers. God said that Israel had too many soldiers for the battle. If they beat the Midianites, they would think they were able to do this because they were great soldiers in sufficient number, not because God was helping them.

God instructed Gideon to tell the soldiers that, if there were any of them who did not want to be there, they could go home. Twenty-two thousand soldiers left and went home, leaving just ten thousand to fight against the Midianites.

God then told Gideon that he still had too many soldiers. God told Gideon to send the soldiers to the river to drink. Now 9,700 scooped up water in their hands to drink, while 300 men lapped up the water as a dog drinks. God told Gideon to send the 9,700 soldiers that scooped up water in their hands home. Gideon would use only the 300 soldiers to fight the 135,000 Midianite soldiers. Now there would be no way that the Israelites could believe they could defeat the Midianites just because they were great soldiers.

Do you think 300 Israelite soldiers versus 135,000 Midianite soldiers was a fair fight? It wasn't because the three hundred Israelite soldiers had the ultimate advantage: God was on their side. God told Gideon to give each of his soldiers a horn and divide them into three companies of one hundred soldiers.

When Gideon gave the signal, the three hundred soldiers blew their horns and yelled, "For the Lord and Gideon!"

As soon as they yelled this, God made it so the 135,000 Midianite soldiers got confused and began to attack each other. The entire Midianite army wiped themselves out. Gideon's army of three hundred did not even have to fight. God did all of the fighting for them. Once again the Israelites were free, and there was peace in the land for forty years.

After Gideon's death, God sent several judges to help Israel after they *once again turned* away from God and had bad things happen to them. One of the judges was the most famous of all, Samson. He actually was not famous; he was infamous. He is well known for doing bad things.

Because Israel did evil things, God allowed the Philistines to conquer them for forty years. God came to a woman named Manaoh who had no children. He told her that she would have a son and he would save Israel from the Philistines. The woman had a son, and she named him Samson. The Spirit of God was within Samson, which caused him to become powerful as he got older.

Once a huge lion attacked Samson. With God's strength in him, he picked up the lion and tore it to pieces. Samson got extremely strong because of God, but he did not always do what God told him to do. He was mischievous, and he would start fights with groups of men when he should not have.

He caused so many problems that his townspeople tried to capture him to turn him over to their enemy, the Philistines, to get rid of him. When they tried to capture Sampson, he picked up the bone of a dead donkey nearby and killed a thousand men with his great strength. This is not what Samson was supposed to do. He was supposed to save his people as a judge from their enemy, not cause problems.

Samson was a married man. However, he got a girlfriend, which was wrong. Her name was Delilah, and she was a troublemaker like Samson. Samson's enemies, the Philistines, came up to her and said they would give her 1,100 pieces of silver if she could find out the secret of Samson's strength so they could capture him.

He told her that, if she tied him up with fresh bowstrings that had not been dried, he would lose his strength. She tied him up with fresh bowstrings when he was sleeping, but he still had his strength. The same thing happened with new ropes that were not used and other fabrics, but they did not work.

Delilah became upset that he was lying to her. She bugged him every day to tell him the secret of his strength. He finally said that, if his hair were cut, all of God's power would leave him.

One day, when Samson fell asleep, Delilah cut his hair. When she did this, all of God's strength left him. She yelled for his enemies, the Philistines. They came in and grabbed him. He tried to get away, but he no longer had any super strength. They tied him up in chains, blinded him, locked him in a prison, and forced him to grind grain.

Over time, Samson's hair began to grow back. God gave Samson his power through his long hair. The Philistines had a party to worship their false god, Dagon. They offered sacrifices to Dagon and thanked him for delivering Samson, their enemy, into their hands. They did not know that Dagon was not a god. God is the only god, and he is the one who gave Samson his power and took away his power because Samson was being bad.

During the Philistine party, they brought Samson out in front of the crowd to tease him and make fun of him. Several thousand Philistines were in the arena. They stood him between two pillars that held up the arena.

Then Samson called to the Lord and said, "O Lord God, please remember me and please strengthen me only this once, O God, that I may be avenged on the Philistines for my two eyes."

Samson put his hand on the pillars to the right and the left of him. He said to God, "Let me die with the Philistines."

Samson pushed each pillar with all his strength, and the arena fell down and killed all of the bad Philistines in it, along with Samson. He killed more of the bad Philistines in this one event than he did during his entire life. His family took Samson's body and buried him.

Israel was once again free and at peace. There were other judges after Samson, and Israel went through periods of good and evil as well as war and peace in the time of the judges.

The Book of Ruth

The book of Ruth is the story of a married older woman who had two sons who were also married. There was a severe famine in the land, and the woman's husband and two sons died. The wife of one of the sons was named Ruth. The older woman said that both of the daughters-in-law could leave her to find new husbands since theirs had died.

Ruth said that she would stay with her mother-in-law because she loved her and she wanted to take care of her. Because Ruth was kind to her mother-in-law, God was kind to Ruth. He gave her a very good man who married her, loved her, and took care of her for the rest of her life.

Chapter 7

The Book of 1 Samuel: Israel's First Kings

There was a man named Samuel, whom God made into a prophet. A prophet is a person who God tells things to, and that person then tells the people what God said. One day, the Israelites were at war with the Philistines. The Philistines defeated the Israelites. When they did, they took the ark of the covenant, the fancy box that held the two tablets with the Ten Commandments on them.

The Philistines took the ark and put it in the temple of their false god, Dagon, next to a big statue of Dagon. When the Philistines woke up the next day, they found the statue of Dagon knocked down on its face before the ark. They put Dagon's statue back up, but the next day they found it on the ground again before the ark with its hands and head cut off. (God did this to show them that he is the only true God.)

The Philistines who lived near where they were storing the ark broke out in tumors. The Philistines moved the ark to the city of Gath. The people there too broke out in tumors, and they panicked. They then moved it to the city of Ekron, and the same thing happened. The Philistines decided to not harden their hearts against the God of Israel (God) like the Egyptians did when they were struck by plagues from God.

They realized that the God of Israel (God) should not be messed with. The sent the ark back to the Israelites. They filled it with gold, as an apology for taking it from then Israelites.

At this time, there were still judges over Israel, like Gideon and Samson. God made Samuel the prophet and then his sons as judges over Israel. Samuel's sons were not honest as judges, and the Israelites became upset over this.

The Israelites came to Samuel and said, "Instead of judges, give us a king to rule over us."

This was against what God wanted. God wanted to be the only king over Israel. However, he told Samuel that, if they wanted a king, they could have a king. He warned them though that they would have problems with a king.

The Israelites told God and Samuel that they wanted a king anyway so they could be like the other countries that had kings. God allowed what the Israelites wanted. God told Samuel to anoint a man named Saul to be their king. Saul was a very tall and handsome man.

When Saul became king of Israel, Israel was at war the Philistines. Saul wanted to get a blessing from God in his fight with the Philistines. The prophet Samuel was supposed to give this blessing to King Saul.

King Saul was impatient. He took matters into his own hands, and he broke some of the commandments and instructions God gave him in doing so. Samuel told King Saul that, because of this, God would remove him from being king. He would anoint another man as king, one who was after God's own heart.

Even after this, King Saul would often not listen to what God wanted him to do. God regretted that he made Saul the king of Israel because he was very disobedient to God. Once again, God had the prophet Samuel tell King Saul that God would replace him with a better king, one who would always do what God told him to do. This greatly upset King Saul.

The prophet Samuel was sad that God rejected Saul as king. God told Samuel that he should not be upset. He sent Samuel to a man named Jesse who lived in Bethlehem. God would make one of Jesse's sons the new king over Israel.

Jesse had many strong, handsome sons. Samuel thought one of these would be chosen as king. God told Samuel that he did not judge people by their appearance; instead he judged people by their heart. (God knows if people are good or bad.)

God chose the youngest of Jesse's sons to be the future king of Israel. He was a shepherd boy, and his name was David. Samuel anointed David to be the future king of Israel. The Spirit of God was with David from that day forward.

David and Goliath

The enemy of Israel at that time, the Philistines, set up a camp on a mountain that was on one side of a valley for their army to battle Israel. The Israelites under King Saul set up their armies on a mountain that was on the other side of this valley. The Philistines sent out their champion soldier named Goliath. He was nine-foot-nine. He had a huge sword and spear, and he was covered in bronze armor.

Goliath yelled out to the Israelites, "Send out your best warrior. If he can beat me, we will be your servants. If I beat him, you will be our servants."

The Israelites had no one to send out to face Goliath. No one in the Israelite army was close to Goliath's size and fierceness.

Goliath came out into the valley and then yelled and cursed at the Israelite army for forty days, challenging them to send a man out to fight him. Three of David's brothers were in Israelite army camp facing the Philistines.

One day, Jesse told his son David to bring some food to his brothers who were fighting the Philistines. When David reached his brothers at the Israelite army camp, he heard Goliath cursing at the Israelite army.

David began to say out loud, "What shall be done for the man who kills this Philistine and takes away the reproach from Israel? For who is this godless Philistine that he should defy the armies of the living God?" (1 Samuel 17:26).

King Saul heard that this boy was questioning about Goliath, so he sent for him. David told King Saul not to worry because he would fight the Philistine. King Saul did not think this was a good idea because David was just a teenager and Goliath was a giant that had been fighting his entire life. David told King Saul that, as a shepherd, lions and bears had taken sheep at times.

David chased the lions and bears down, got into battles with them, killed them, and saved the sheep. He told him that he would do the same to Goliath, the godless Philistine giant, because he defied the armies of the living God.

King Saul said to David, "Go, and the Lord be with you!" (1 Samuel 17:37).

When David went out to fight Goliath, he wore no armor. The only weapon he had was a slingshot and five smooth stones that he took from a stream. When Goliath saw David coming out to fight him, he was insulted that the Israelites would send out a boy to fight a great champion like himself.

Goliath began to curse at David and the Israelites. David said to Goliath,

> You come to me with a sword and with a spear and with a javelin, but I come to you in the name of the Lord of hosts, the God of the armies of Israel, whom you have defied. This day the Lord will deliver you into my hand, and I will strike you down. All the earth will know that there is a God in Israel, for the battle is the Lord's, and he will give you into our hand. (1 Samuel 17:45–47)

When Goliath approached to meet David, David ran quickly at Goliath. David pulled a stone out of his bag, put in in his slingshot, and slung it at

Goliath. The stone hit Goliath in the forehead so hard that it sunk into his head. Goliath fell facedown on the ground and was dead.

David defeated the Philistine giant, Goliath, without a sword, just with the power of God behind him. When the Philistines saw what happened, they became very afraid and ran away from the Israelites.

After David defeated Goliath, King Saul moved David into the king's castle with him. There, God made it so that King Saul's son, Jonathan, became best friends with David. King Saul sent David into every battle of the Israelite army. Because God was with David, the Israelites won every battle that David was a part of. This caused King Saul to make David in charge of the Israelite armies.

One day after David won a battle, the women of Israel were singing in the streets, "Saul has struck down his thousands, and David his ten thousands" (1 Samuel 18:7). This meant that the people believed that David was a greater warrior than King Saul was. This made King Saul jealous of David from that day on.

The next day, a spirit sent by God tormented King Saul. (Remember, God had rejected Saul as king of Israel because he disobeyed God several times in the past.) While King Saul was irritated, on two occasions, he picked up a spear and threw it at David with the intentions to kill him. Each time, David ducked out of the way.

King Saul repeatedly tried to kill David because he was jealous of him. King Saul's son, Jonathan, was David's best friend. Whenever he heard that his father was going to try to kill David, he would warn David so he could escape.

One day, David entered a church and asked for food for he and his men and a sword for himself. The head priest gave David these things because he knew David was a good man. He did not know that King Saul was trying to kill David.

When King Saul heard that the priests helped David, he killed eighty-five priests that worked at the church and everyone in the whole town. King Saul was becoming extremely evil. He was trying to hold on to his power as king even though God rejected him. He was now killing everyone that he felt got in his way. On two occasions, David had King Saul trapped as they faced each other, and David could have killed him.

Each time, however, David let King Saul go. He said that it was God who anointed Saul as king, and David should never lay a hand against someone God anointed. He believed that, when God decided it was time for Saul to stop being king, he would get rid of Saul himself.

King Saul twice thanked David for sparing his life, and he said he would no longer come after David. However, his promises to leave David alone never lasted long. He was overcome quickly by his envy of David.

Around this same time, the prophet Samuel died and went to heaven. The Israelites were presently fighting with the Philistines. King Saul tried to ask God what he should do in battles. God would not answer King Saul because Saul kept doing very bad things. So King Saul went to a fortune-teller and asked her to contact the prophet Samuel, who was in heaven, to ask him what to do in battle.

God said we should never go to fortune-tellers because they get their powers from evil spirits, not God. The fortune-teller contacted Samuel, and Samuel was mad that King Saul did this. Samuel told King Saul that, because he kept doing bad things, God said that he would die tomorrow in a battle with the Philistines.

That is exactly what happened. The next day, King Saul and his forces were in a battle with the Philistines. King Saul was killed, along with his son Jonathan, who was David's best friend.

Book 2 of Samuel

David was brought the news that King Saul and his son, Jonathan, who was his best friend, were killed in battle with the Philistines. This made

David very sad. After King Saul's death, David was anointed king over part of Israel, while another man named Ish-bosheth was anointed king over another part of Israel.

A battle ensued between family members of Saul and David to determine who would follow King Saul as king over all of Israel. Eventually Israel anointed David as king over all of their country, and God said this would happen when he had Samuel anoint him as future king when he was a shepherd boy. David was thirty years old when he became king of Israel, and he ruled as king for forty years.

When David became king of Israel, the ark with the Ten Commandments inside of it was sitting in a tent. King David said to Nathan the prophet, "I live in a house of cedar wood, yet the ark of God is only in a tent."

David wanted to build a temple for the ark. The prophet Nathan asked God if King David should build a temple for the ark. God told Nathan to tell King David that it was ok for the ark to be in a tent up to this point because it could be easily moved around to wherever the Israelites were.

God said that one of David's sons who would be king (future King Solomon) would be the one who would build a beautiful temple for the ark. As for King David, God said that he would make King David a great name for all eternity. He would protect him and Israel from their enemies so they would not bother them. King David's descendants would last forever, and the kingdom of Israel under David's name would also last forever.

This came true. The Jewish people are still here. Additionally the flag of the country of Israel today is a white flag with a big six-pointed star in the middle of it, which is called the Star of David.

From this point on, David's armies defeated anyone that tried to attack Israel. David was a kind, honest, and fair king. God said that King David was a man after his own heart. Everything was going very well for David and Israel because David was a good man that followed whatever God said … until David committed a great sin. At that point, things fell apart for King David because he did something very evil and sinful.

David and Bathsheba

One day, King David stayed back at his palace while his armies were out in battle. He was walking across the rooftop of his palace when he looked down and noticed a very beautiful woman named Bathsheba, the wife of Uriah the Hittite, one of David's best soldiers and a very good man.

David had Bathsheba brought to him. He slept with her, which was a great sin because she was not his wife. She was the wife of Uriah. Shortly after, Bathsheba informed David that she was pregnant with his baby. David tried to cover this up. He brought Uriah home from the battle and told him to spend some time with Bathsheba because he deserved it for being such a good soldier.

Uriah was a man of good character. He refused to do so. He asked, "How can I spend time in comfort when my soldiers are fighting in a battle?"

He would not go to his wife, Bathsheba. Instead he slept on the ground in front of King David's palace. When David saw that he could not cover up his sin by making Bathsheba's baby look like it was her husband's, he decided to kill Uriah. David wrote a sealed message and gave it to Uriah himself to deliver to the generals.

The sealed message said that, when they were in a fierce battle, they were to put Uriah at the front of the battle. Then the soldiers were instructed to back away and leave Uriah by himself in the battle so he would be killed.

This is what happened. After Uriah was killed in battle, as King David had ordered, King David then took Uriah's wife, Bathsheba, and made her his own wife. This angered God greatly.

God sent the prophet Nathan to tell King David that God knew all about the series of evil sins that David had committed against Bathsheba, Uriah, and God himself. David crumbled in the presence of the prophet Nathan when he told him that God knew about everything that he did.

God told the prophet Nathan to tell King David that, from this point on, he would constantly have trouble in his life. The son he would have with Bathsheba would die shortly after birth. He would have strife continually within his own household. One of his own sons would try to kill him, and he would no longer have any peace.

David was very sorry for the sins he had committed against God, Uriah, and Bathsheba. He repented and asked God for forgiveness. God forgave David, and he no longer held his sins against him. However, he now had to deal with the consequences that his grave sins caused. He would struggle with problems in his life for as long as he would live.

David had another son with Bathsheba. He named him Solomon, and he would be the future king of Israel after King David died. David also had a son, Amnon, and a daughter, Tamar. Amnon horribly mistreated his half-sister Tamar and hurt her very badly. This made their half-brother, Absalom, very angry. At one point, Absalom killed Amnon for badly hurting Tamar. This whole series of incidents made their father, King David, very sad.

After Absalom killed his brother, he ran to another country and hid from the law for three years. After three years, King David allowed Absalom to return home to Jerusalem. However, when Absalom returned, his father, King David, mishandled the situation. He ignored Absalom and refused to speak to him. This caused Absalom to grow to hate his father, King David.

Absalom's hatred for his father increased over time. He became power hungry, and he wanted to get rid of his father, King David, so he could become king. Absalom began to tell lies to the people, making himself look good and his father, King David, look bad.

Many people believed these lies, and they began to follow Absalom as their leader instead of King David. At one point, King David and his friends had to flee their castle because they were afraid that Absalom would attack it and try to kill the king.

Sure enough, Absalom brought an army with him, and they invaded King David's castle in Jerusalem with the intent to kill him so he could be king. David ran away before this so he was not there when Absalom invaded and tried to kill him.

King David gathered his army, and Absalom gathered his army. And they went into battle with each other. During the battle, Absalom was killed. Even though Absalom was trying to kill his father, King David was extremely sad when he heard of the death of his son because he was his son and he loved him.

All of the tragedies that King David went through were consequences of his series of sins of killing Uriah and stealing his wife, Bathsheba:

- His son with Bathsheba died at birth.
- His son Amnon hurt his daughter Tamar.
- Another son, Absalom, killed Amnon, his brother, because of this.
- Absalom tried to kill King David, and he himself was killed.

King David lost his peace as the consequence of willfully engaging in serious sins.

Chapter 8

Israel's Next Group of Kings and Prophets

Book of 1 and 2 Kings

When King David was very old, he anointed one of his sons to be the next king of Israel after him. His son's name was Solomon. Solomon was another son that King David had with Bathsheba now that she was his wife.

King David told Solomon to be a good man and to follow the ways of God. King David died, and Solomon took his place as king. One night, God appeared to King Solomon in a dream. He told King Solomon to ask him for whatever he wanted, and God would give it to him. King Solomon said that, because God made him king, he asked God to give him wisdom to be a good king for the Israelites and so he would always make good decisions as their king.

This pleased God that Solomon asked him for this. God said,

> Because you have asked this, and have not asked for yourself long life or riches or the life of your enemies, but have asked for yourself understanding to discern what is right, behold, I now do according to your word. Behold, I give you a wise and discerning mind, so that none like

you has been before you and none like you shall arise after you. I give you also what you have not asked, both riches an honor, so that no other king shall compare with you, all your days. *And if you walk in my ways, keeping my statutes and my commandments, as your father David walked, then I will lengthen your days.* (1 Kings 3:10–14)

God greatly blessed King Solomon. He was the wisest man in the world at the time, and he had great riches. People from different nations came to Israel to hear King Solomon speak because of his wisdom. God instructed King Solomon to build him a temple. Solomon gathered almost 200,000 men to work to help build the temple for God in Israel.

It took Solomon seven years to build the temple, and it was very fancy and beautiful. King Solomon then built a palace for himself, which took thirteen years to build. This was also fancy and beautiful. Solomon brought the ark of the covenant and put it in the temple.

As soon as King Solomon finished building a temple for God, God appeared to Solomon. He told King Solomon that, if he were a man who followed God with integrity of heart and uprightness, doing whatever God commanded him to and keeping God's laws and rules, then God would establish Solomon's royal throne over Israel forever, as he promised Solomon's father, King David.

However, God warned King Solomon that, if he turned away from following God or his children did not keep God's commandments and his laws that he set before King Solomon, but went and served other gods and worshiped them, then God would cut off Israel from the land that he had given them. He would cast the temple out of his sight, and Israel would be cursed by all peoples. Solomon's palace would become a heap of ruins.

People would ask why God did this to Israel and to King Solomon's house. And they would say, "Because Israel abandoned the Lord their God who brought their fathers out of Egypt and served other gods instead, and therefore God has brought disaster on them" (1 Kings 9:9).

One day, the queen of Sheba heard of the great riches and blessings that God had given King Solomon. So she took a journey to visit King Solomon to see if the reports were true. She asked King Solomon very difficult questions. He was able to answer every one beyond her expectations.

The wealth and blessings that God had given King Solomon took the queen of Sheba's breath away. King Solomon and the queen of Sheba exchanged gifts. The queen of Sheba went back to her own land and told everyone about the great wisdom and riches that God had given to King Solomon.

Despite King Solomon being the wisest man in the world, he started to not listen to what God told him to do. God told Solomon to not marry any women who did not follow God because she would pull Solomon away from God. Also a man was supposed to have only one wife. Solomon had seven hundred wives and three hundred girlfriends. Many of these wives did not follow God, and they pulled King Solomon away from following God.

Over time, Solomon started to worship the false gods that some of his wives worshipped. Some of these gods involved demon worship, which included extremely evil things, such as human sacrifices.

What King Solomon did greatly angered God. God said that, because Solomon disobeyed God and was worshiping false gods and demons, God would take eleven out of the twelve kingdoms that King Solomon now ruled out of the hands of his son in the future. Other people would rule them.

Up until this point, King Solomon had total peace in his kingdom. Because he was now acting badly, God took away his protection of King Solomon. This allowed a lot of enemies of King Solomon to rise up and give him trouble.

King Solomon ruled Israel for forty years. He started out following God, and all went well for him. He turned away from following God, and he then had major problems. King Solomon died, and his son, Rehoboam, replaced him as king of Israel.

Rehoboam was an evil king who was mean to the people of Israel. This caused many of the Israelites to rebel against King Rehoboam, and the country was greatly divided. Many other kings of Israel followed King Rehoboam. Some were good; others were evil. God blessed the good ones, and things went well for them. The bad kings had many problems while they were kings. God did not help them because they refused to follow him.

Elijah

God raised up a prophet named Elijah. God gave Elijah the power to do mighty miracles so the people would believe that he was a prophet sent by God. At this time, many of the people of Israel were following God. However, many of the Israelites were following a false god named Baal. Some people were following both God and Baal.

Elijah said to the people, "How long will you people go back and forth deciding which god to follow? If God is the real God, then follow him. If Baal is the real God, then follow him."

Elijah put the followers of Baal to a test in front of the Israelite people to see who the real god was, God or Baal. He said, "I am the only prophet of God here, but Baal has four hundred and fifty men here who are prophets of Baal. Let's have a contest. I will kill a bull, and the four hundred and fifty prophets of Baal will kill a bull. We will each put our bull on a pile of wood. The prophets of Baal can call out to Baal to send fire down from the sky to set their bull and wood on fire, and I will call out to God to send down fire from the sky to set their bull and wood on fire. Whichever God does this is the true God."

The prophets of Baal and the people of Israel agreed to this. The 450 prophets of Baal went first. They killed a bull, put it on a big pile of wood, and cried out to Baal from morning until noon for him to send fire down from the sky. They yelled for so long that they were losing their voices and were limping. Nothing happened.

Elijah said to them, "Cry out loud, for he is a god. Either he is goofing off, he is going to the bathroom, he is on a journey, or perhaps he is asleep and must be awakened."

They ranted and raved on until later in the day. By this point, they were passing out from exhaustion from crying out to Baal, but absolutely nothing happened.

Elijah now called the people of Israel over to his pile of wood with a bull on it. He laid twelve stones around his pile, representing the twelve tribes of Israel. He then had the people completely soak his pile of wood and the bull with water, so it would be impossible for a person to set it on fire.

Then Elijah said,

> Oh Lord, the God of Abraham, Isaac and Jacob (Israel), let it be known this day that you are God in Israel, and that I am your servant, and that I have done all these things at your word. Answer me, O Lord, answer me, that this people may know that you, O Lord, are God, and that you have turned their hearts back. (1 Kings 19:36–37)

As soon as Elijah finished saying this, God rained down an immense fire from heaven on the bull, wood, and water, and it burned everything up. When the people saw it, they fell on their faces and said, "The Lord, he is God; The Lord, he is God" (1 Kings 18:39). Elijah had the people grab the prophets of the false god Baal and get rid of them.

The prophet Elijah got an assistant, Elisha, to help him. God gave the power to Elijah to do many miracles so the people would believe he was a prophet of God. One day, God told Elijah that he would take him up to heaven while he was still alive.

Before he was taken, Elijah asked Elisha if he could do anything for him before God took him to heaven. Elisha asked Elijah if he could give him a double portion of his spirit.

Elijah said that was up to God to do, but it was ok with him if God did that. While they were talking, God sent down chariots of fire and horses of fire that separated the two of them. God then took Elijah up to heaven in a whirlwind (like a tornado) while he was still alive.

Elijah was one of the only people in the Bible who did not have to die to go to heaven. God brought him up there while he was still alive. When he went up to heaven, a double portion of his spirit was given to Elisha, like he asked. Now Elisha also had the power to do great miracles.

The miracles god gave Elisha the power to:

- cause food to keep appearing in a poor woman's house in an abundance to prevent her from starving so she could sell it to buy her sons out of slavery;
- make it so a childless woman gave birth to a son;
- bring a boy back to life who had died;
- remove the poison from poisoned food so the people could eat it; and
- heal a man of leprosy.

Once the king of Syria was at war with Israel. He wanted to capture the prophet Elisha because Elisha was able to warn Israel that Syria would attack them because God would tell him this. The king of Syria sent an army and surrounded Elijah and his friends. God sent an army of soldiers, horses, and chariots of fire from heaven to protect Elisha. The king of Syria and his armies saw this and never went after Elisha again.

During this period of time, there were many good kings over Israel, but even more bad ones who did not follow what God instructed them to do. They ignored God's instructions and did what they wanted to do. Sometimes their actions were very sinful.

Eventually God ran out of patience with these bad kings of Israel. Since the kings of Israel did not want to follow God's instructions, he took his help and protection away from Israel. This allowed Israel to be totally defeated by a very powerful king of the country of Babylon named Nebuchadnezzar. He led the remaining Israelites that were still alive after he conquered them to captivity as exiles in his kingdom of Babylon. After this, God allowed the Israelites to be transitioned into being under the rule of the Chaldeans or the Persians.

The Book of Ezra

During the time the Chaldeans held the Israelites captive in Persia, the Persians had a king named Cyrus. God stirred the spirit of King Cyrus to help the Israelites and set them free. He made a proclamation that the Israelites could return to Israel and rebuild the Temple of God where they had worshipped him. Nebuchadnezzar of Babylon destroyed the temple when his army conquered Israel.

Once the temple was rebuilt, God sent a prophet named Ezra to teach the Israelites about God. God warned the people not to marry foreign people who did not believe in God, but once again, they did it anyway.

The Book of Nehemiah

While the Israelites were still captives of the Babylonians and Chaldeans, God sent a man named Nehemiah to the king of the Babylonians to ask permission to return to Jerusalem in Israel to repair their damaged walls. God influenced the king of Babylon to allow Nehemiah and his men to do this. Slowly the king of Babylon allowed many of the Israelites to return to live in Israel. However, the kings of Babylon still ruled them.

Chapter 9

The Book of Esther

In the book of Esther, the king of Babylon, Persia, and Media ruled the Israelites. The king's name at that time was King Ahasuerus. The king had a huge party for the army, the princes, and the governors of the kingdom that lasted for many days.

After seven days of partying, the king ordered that his queen, Queen Vashti, be brought to the party to show her off to everyone there because she was very beautiful. Queen Vashti refused to come as the king ordered.

King Ahasuerus became enraged that the queen refused his order to come to the party. The king consulted his consultants on how to handle this. They said that the queen needed to be replaced by another woman as queen for disobeying the king. So Queen Vashti had her title as queen removed. Beautiful women from all over the land were brought to the king so he could select a new queen.

There was a good Jewish man named Mordecai. He was living in the kingdom ruled by King Ahasuerus. He was raising up a young woman named Esther. Esther's parents died when she was young. Mordecai was an older cousin of Esther, and he adopted her as his own daughter because she had no parents.

Esther was a very beautiful young woman. When the king's order was sent out to bring beautiful women to the palace to select a new queen, Esther was brought to the palace along with many other women.

Esther was the nicest and most beautiful of all the women brought to the palace. Over time, she became the favorite of King Ahasuerus, and he eventually made her queen to replace Queen Vashti, who had disobeyed him. Each day during this time, Esther's father, Mordecai, would walk in front of the palace to find out how Esther was doing and what was happening to her.

Esther did not tell anyone that she was Jewish and from Israel because Mordecai told her not to. One day, when Mordecai was standing at the king's gate to hear how Esther was doing that day, two of the king's servants became angry with the king and were making plans to hurt him. Mordecai overheard this. Mordecai told Queen Esther, his daughter, who then told the king what Mordecai discovered. The two men were arrested for trying to hurt the king. Mordecai saved the king's life.

There was an official in this kingdom named Haman. The king promoted Haman to be second-in-charge in the kingdom behind the king. Everyone whom Haman passed had to bow down to Haman under the king's orders. Mordecai would never bow down to Haman. He said that he was Jewish, and under Jewish law, God was the only person that people should bow down to. ("Jewish" people was a name given to the people of Israel. Remember, they were captured and living in this other country at this time.)

Haman became very angry at this. He decided that, not only would he kill Mordecai for not bowing down to him, he would kill every Jewish person in the whole kingdom!

Haman went to the king and said, "There are a bunch of people living in this kingdom called the Jews. They are not following all of your laws and commands, and I think it would be in the best interest of the kingdom if they be destroyed."

The king said, "Do whatever you think is the right thing to do with them."

Haman sent out a letter to all the officials of the kingdom that, on December 13, all of the Jews in the kingdom were to be killed. Mordecai heard about this plan, and he was extremely upset. Mordecai told his daughter, Queen Esther, that Haman planned to kill all of the Jewish people in the kingdom and even her because she was Jewish.

Esther sent a message to all of the Jews in the kingdom to fast (not eat or drink anything) for three days and to keep praying to God to save them. Esther came up with a plan to save her people.

Queen Esther went to the king and asked if a banquet could be held. He was to make sure that Haman was there. The king agreed. Haman was happy that he was invited to this banquet. He was talking to his wife about it. She reminded him that Mordecai would not bow down to him and suggested that a seventy-five-foot pole be put up and Mordecai would be hanged on it at the banquet. Haman agreed.

The night before the banquet, the king could not sleep. (God caused this to happen). He asked that his servants read to him reports of things that happened recently in the kingdom. In the reports, he discovered that Mordecai saved his life by discovering that two of his servants were planning to kill the king.

The king asked, "What was done to reward Mordecai for saving my life?"

"Nothing," they replied.

The king called in Haman, who had just finished building the seventy-five-foot pole to hang Mordecai.

The king asked Haman, "What should be done to honor a man that I like?"

Haman assumed the king was going to honor him. He said, "Put the king's robes on the man, put him on the king's horse, put the king's crown on his head, and parade him through the city saying, 'This is what happens to a man that the king honors.'"

Then the king said, "That is a great idea. Do all that for Mordecai the Jew because he saved my life and I want to honor him."

Haman became terrified. He did all of those great things for Mordecai: he put the king's robes on him, put him on a horse with the king's crown on his head, and paraded Mordecai through the streets saying, "This is what happens to a man that the king honors."

Haman then ran and hid because the king now loved Mordecai and Haman was trying to kill him.

At the banquet, Queen Esther told the king that Haman planned not only to kill Mordecai, who saved the king's life, but all of the Jewish people. She said she was also a Jew. The king became enraged at Haman. The king was told that Haman had just built a seventy-five-foot pole and planned to hang Mordecai on it that day.

The king said, "Oh really? Well, go and hang Haman on that pole that he built to kill my friend Mordecai."

So Haman was hanged on that pole, and Mordecai and Queen Esther saved the Jews from destruction. The king stopped all of the plans that Haman set to kill all the Jews on December 13. Because Mordecai saved the king's life, he was promoted to a very powerful position in the kingdom, and everyone in the land loved him.

Chapter 10

The Book of Job

Job was a man that had great faith in God. He worshipped God daily and always followed God's instructions. Job was also the richest and most successful man in the East. He had abundant land, herds of animals, possessions, and seven sons and three daughters.

One day, God and Satan were having a conversation. God asked Satan what he had been doing lately. Satan said he had been roaming the earth, observing things. God asked Satan what he thought about Job. He said that Job was the most blameless and upright man on earth. He feared God and turned away from evil.

Satan said that Job was only good to God because God protected Job and all he had. He also blessed Job so that everything he did was successful. Satan said that, if this protection and blessings were taken away and very difficult trials hit him, he would curse God to his face. God said he would take his protections and blessings away from Job so Satan could test him. God put one restriction on Satan: he could not touch Job himself.

Satan caused horrible tragedies to hit Job, so he lost all of his treasures in one day. Two different groups of robbers attacked properties that Job owned, taking all of his possessions and killing the people that worked there. Satan caused fire to come down from the sky and burn up a farm he owned, killing his animals and the people that worked for him. Finally a huge wind knocked down a house that his ten children were in, killing all of them. In all of this, Job did not curse God to his face, as Satan said he would, and he still worshipped God.

Satan and God met and had another conversation about this. God told Satan that, even after he caused all of these terrible tragedies to happen to Job, Job still worshipped and followed God. Satan said that was because nothing actually bad happened to Job. Bad things happened to Job's possessions and the people around him.

Satan said, if something bad happened to Job, he would curse God to his face. God told Satan that he would remove his protection from Job himself so Satan could test him. Satan caused loathsome sores to appear from the sole of Job's feet to the top of Job's head.

These horrible sores, along with losing all of the things Job had in his life, pushed Job over the edge. Job quickly went into a downward spiral of anger and hopelessness. First, he wished that he was never born. Next, he wished that God would kill him so he would not have to go through this horrible grief. Then he got angry at God, saying that he never did anything wrong and he did not deserve for these things to happen to him.

Next, he said that God was an unfair God and that he did these bad things to him when he should not have because Job thought he was so good. (He did not realize that Satan, not God, did these things to him.) Then he said that God was actually an evil God who favored evil people over good people.

He said that God did not cause tragedies to hit evil people like he caused to hit him. God must favor evil people over good people. Next, Job said that he wished that he himself were an evil person. He said that evil people had it good in life. They did not experience the tragedies that he was, so he wished that he were an evil person.

Finally, Job's hidden pride was exposed. He said that what he missed most about losing everything was not losing his kids or being separated from God. It was that he used to be an important big shot that everyone looked up to. That was what he wanted back more than anything.

At this point, God appeared to Job. He reminded Job that God was God and Job was not God. God created everything that existed. Everything Job had was because God created it and gave it to him. It was not right that Job was acting like the things that he lost were things that he himself created and were rightfully his. They were gifts from God.

In the presence of God, Job became humbled. He asked God for forgiveness for his arrogance and for turning against God in his trial. God forgave Job. He also restored Job. He doubled all of the possessions that Satan took away. Additionally, he gave Job ten more children. These children were the most beautiful children in all of the land. Job lived to a happy, ripe-old age, and he died in peace.

The Book of Psalms

The book of Psalms is a very dense and complicated book. They are verses written mostly by King David that chronicled his life experiences and prayers to God. I would not be able to give it justice if I summarized it. Therefore, please read it on your own if possible.

Chapter 11

The Book of Proverbs

King Solomon, the son of King David of Israel, whom God made the wisest man who ever lived, wrote the book of Proverbs. But the real author of everything in the Bible is God. He guided Solomon on what to write.

I wanted to include some of the proverbs from the book of Proverbs in this Bible summary because they help teach us how God wants us to live. Additionally it will give you an idea about what the book of Proverbs in the Bible is like. It would benefit you greatly to read the entire book of Proverbs for yourself. They truly are gems of wisdom that you can benefit from in your daily life. All of the following proverbs were taken from the book of Proverbs:

- "My son, do not despise the Lord's discipline or be wary of his reproof, for the Lord disciplines who he loves, as a father the son in whom he delights."
- "The fear of the Lord is the hatred of evil."
- "God loves those who love him, and those who seek God diligently find him."
- "A wise son makes a glad father, but a foolish son is a sorrow to his mother."
- "Treasures gained by wickedness do not profit, but righteousness delivers you from death."
- "Hatred stirs up problems, but love covers all offenses."

- "What the wicked dreads will come upon him, but the desire of the righteous will be granted."
- "When pride comes, then comes disgrace, but with the humble people is wisdom."
- "The righteous is delivered from trouble, and the wicked walks into it instead."
- "Whoever criticizes his neighbor lacks sense, but a person of understanding remains silent."
- "One gives to others generously, yet grows richer, another withholds what he should give and is always poor." (God blesses and helps those who are generous to others.)
- "Whoever trusts in his riches will fall, but those who trust in God will prosper."
- "A person who is kind benefits himself, but a cruel person hurts himself."
- "Be assured, an evil person will not go unpunished, but the children of the righteous will be delivered."
- "The desire of the righteous ends only in good; the expectation of the wicked in wrath."
- "Whoever brings blessing will be enriched, and one who waters will himself be watered."
- "Whoever loves discipline loves knowledge, but he who hates being corrected is stupid."
- "A good person obtains favor from the Lord, but a person of evil devices is condemned by God."
- "The way of a fool is right in his own eyes, but a wise man listens to advice."
- "Whoever guards his mouth preserves his life; but he who opens wide his lips comes to ruin."
- "Whoever despises the Word of God brings destruction on himself, but he who reveres the commandments will be rewarded."
- "Whoever walks with the wise will become wise, but the companion of fools will suffer harm."
- "The righteous has enough to satisfy his appetite, but the belly of the wicked always wants more."

- "Leave the presence of a fool, for there you do not meet the words of knowledge."
- "One who is wise is cautious and turns away from evil, but a fool is reckless and careless."
- "Whoever despises his neighbor is a sinner, but blessed is he who is generous to the poor."
- "In all work there is profit, but mere talk leads only to poverty."
- "In the fear of the Lord one has strong confidence, and his children will have a place of safety."
- "Whoever is slow to anger has great understanding, but he who has a hasty temper is a fool."
- "A peaceful heart gives life to the body, but envy makes the bones rot."
- "Whoever oppresses a poor person insults the poor person's Maker, which is God. But he who is generous to the needy honors God."
- "A soft answer turns away wrath, but harsh words stirs up anger."
- "The sacrifice of the wicked is an abomination to the Lord, but the prayer of the upright is acceptable to him."
- "Better is a little with love for God then great treasure, but problems due to having no love for God."
- "Better is a dinner of just salad where love is, than a full course meal and hatred with it."
- "Without counsel plans fail, but with many advisers they succeed."
- "Whoever is greedy for unjust gain troubles his own household, but he who hates bribes will live."
- "The Lord is far from the wicked, but he hears the prayers of the righteous."
- "Whoever ignores instruction despises himself, but he who listens to correction gains intelligence."
- "It is better to have a little with righteousness than a lot of money with injustice."
- "How much better to get wisdom than gold! To get understanding is to be chosen rather than silver."
- "Pride goes before destruction, and a haughty spirit before a fall."
- "It is better to be of a lowly spirit with the poor than to divide riches with the proud."

- "Whoever gives thought to God's word will discover good, and blessed is the person who trusts in the Lord."
- "Whoever is slow to anger is better than the mighty, and he who rules his spirit is better than he who rules a city."
- "A joyful heart is good medicine, but a crushed spirit dries up the bones."
- "A false witness will not go unpunished, and he who breathes out lies will not escape."
- "Whoever is generous to the poor lends to the Lord, and God will repay him for his good deed."
- "Do not say 'I will repay evil.' Wait for the Lord and he will deliver you."
- "To do righteousness and justice is more acceptable to the Lord than sacrifice."
- "Whoever closes his ear to the cry of the poor will himself call out someday and not be answered."
- "Whoever pursues righteousness and kindness will find life, righteousness, and honor."
- "A good name is to be chosen rather than great riches, and favor is better than silver or gold."
- "The rich and the poor will meet together; the Lord is the maker of them all."
- "The reward for humility and fear of the Lord is riches and honor and life."
- "Do not envy sinners, but continue to love the Lord always."
- "Never say 'I will do bad to him as he has done to me; I will get back at the person for what he has done.'"
- "If your enemy is hungry, give him something to eat. If he is thirsty, give him something to drink. For this will make him ashamed about being your enemy, and the Lord will reward you."
- "Due to a lack of wood a fire goes out, and where there is no gossiping, fighting stops."
- "Let another praise you; do not praise yourself."
- "The cautious sees danger and hides himself, but the foolish walk into it and suffer for it."
- "Iron sharpens iron, and one man sharpens another."

- "The wicked flee when no one pursues, but the righteous are as bold as a lion."
- "Better is a poor man who walks in his integrity than a rich man who is crooked in his ways."
- "Whoever misleads upright people into an evil way will fall into his own pit, but the blameless will have a godly inheritance."
- "Whoever hides his wrongdoings will not prosper, but he who confesses and stops doing them will receive mercy."
- "One's pride will bring him low, but he who is humble in spirit will obtain honor."
- "Give me neither poverty nor riches; If I am rich, I may say 'Who needs God?'"
- "If I am poor, I may steal and dishonor the name of my God."

Chapter 12

The Book of Daniel

When God allowed the Babylonians (Chaldeans) to conquer Israel because Israel kept going against what God told them to do, the Israelites were taken away as captives to the land of Babylon. When they got there, they were educated for three years in the customs of the Chaldeans. After that, they would stand before the king to see if they were worthy to become part of the Chaldean society. During these three years, they were given daily servings of Chaldean food and drink.

A young man from Israel living as a Babylonian exile was named Daniel. Daniel refused to eat the king's food and drinks because God prohibited some of the food he was given for the Jews to not eat. The king's servants said to Daniel that, if he did not eat the king's food given to him, he would become weak and sick and they would get in trouble because it would look like they were not feeding Daniel.

Daniel told the king's servants to test him and his three friends for ten days. He told them to just give them vegetables and water for ten days. At the end of ten days, the king's servants would inspect their health. If they were healthy, then they didn't have to eat the king's food. If they were not healthy, then they would eat the king's food. The king's servants agreed to this.

At the end of ten days, Daniel and his three friends were healthier than all of the other young men there were. That is because God was taking care of them because they followed God. God gave Daniel and his three friends great wisdom, which the king eventually discovered. The king often asked them for advice on important matters, and their advice was better than that of the other men in the kingdom.

At one point, King Nebuchadnezzar had a troublesome dream. He put out an order to all of the wise men in the kingdom of Babylon that he wanted them not to just interpret what his dream meant, but to also tell him what his secret dream was. He did this to see if the wise men truly had special abilities and to prevent them from fabricating any interpretation of his dream. No one could tell the king what his dream was. Because Daniel was obedient to God, God allowed Daniel to tell the king of the dream that he had and its interpretation.

Because he was the only one of the king's wise men who could do this, the king made Daniel ruler over the whole province of Babylon and chief prefect over all of the wise men of Babylon. In turn, Daniel appointed his three friends—Shadrach, Meshach, and Abednego—over all the affairs of the Babylon province.

Daniel's Friends and the Fiery Furnace

One day, King Nebuchadnezzar, the king of Babylon, made a golden statue ninety feet high and nine feet wide. King Nebuchadnezzar commanded all of the people of Babylon that they were to fall on their knees and worship the statue whenever the king would blow a horn or play music. It was reported to the king that Daniel's three friends would not bow down and worship the golden statue whenever the king blew a horn or played music.

The names of Daniel's three friends were Shadrach, Meshach, and Abednego. The king became extremely angry. He brought Shadrach, Meshach, and Abednego to his palace. He told them that, if they did not bow down and worship the golden statue whenever the king played music or blew a horn, they would be thrown into a fiery furnace.

The three men said to the king, "Our God is able to deliver us from your fiery furnace. But even if he does not, wed will not serve your gods or worship the golden statue that you set up" (Daniel 3:16–18).

The king went into an angry rage when they said this. He ordered that the furnace be heated seven times hotter than usual. He ordered soldiers to tie up Shadrach, Meshach, and Abednego and throw them into the burning fiery furnace. When the soldiers tied the three men up and threw them into the furnace, the fire was so hot that it killed the soldiers that threw them into the fire.

As King Nebuchadnezzar looked on, he jumped up in astonishment. He said to his followers, "Did we not cast three men bound into the fire?"

They said, "Yes, we did, King."

The king said, "But I see four men, untied walking around in the middle of the fire, and they are not hurt; and the appearance of the fourth one is like the son of God" (Daniel 3:24–25).

(Jesus himself came and made it so the fire did not hurt them, and he was in there with them!)

King Nebuchadnezzar came close to the fiery furnace and yelled, "Shadrach, Meshach, and Abednego, servants of the Most High God, come out and come here!" (Daniel 3:26). The three men came out of the fire, and everyone saw that the fire did not hurt them at all.

King Nebuchadnezzar then said, "Blessed be the God of Shadrach, Meshach and Abednego, who has come and saved these three men who trusted in Him, and ignored my command and risked their lives rather than serve and worship any god except their own God" (Daniel 3:28).

King Nebuchadnezzar then made a law that no one could speak anything bad against the God of these three men (our God) because their God is the only true God. Additionally Shadrach, Meshach, and Abednego were promoted to very important positions in Babylon. God used these three men to convince the king of Babylon that our God is the only true God.

Daniel and the Lion's Den

God helped Daniel in many ways because Daniel listened to God and followed what he said to do in his life. Daniel rose to a high position in the Babylonian government because of this. The other leaders of the government became jealous of Daniel. They were searching for a way to get him in trouble so they could get rid of him. They convinced King Darius to make a law that, for thirty days, no one should ask any god for help with anything or pray to any god. If they did, he or she would be thrown into a lion's den. They did this because they knew that Daniel prayed to God every day. The king agreed to this. He did not know they were trying to get rid of Daniel, whom the king liked.

When Daniel heard about this new law, he got down on his knees and prayed to God like he usually did. The men who were jealous of Daniel were spying on him, knowing that he prayed to God every day.

When they saw him praying to God, they went to the king and said, "King Darius, did you not make a law that, if anyone prayed to any god over this thirty-day period, he would be thrown in a lions' den?"

The king said, "Yes, I did agree to that law."

The jealous men said to the king, "Daniel, who is one of the captives from Israel, pays no attention to you or your law because we saw him praying to his God three times every day."

The king was very upset about this because he liked Daniel. He tried to save Daniel from being thrown into a lions' den. However in that culture, when a king makes a law, it could not then be changed, even by the king himself. These evil men tricked the king into making this law. Daniel was cast into the lions' den.

Before he went in, the king said to Daniel, "May your God, who you serve continually, deliver you from the lions!"

A big stone was placed over the entrance of the lions' den so Daniel could not escape. The king went back to his castle and fasted from food and drink all night, hoping that Daniel's God (our God) would save him.

In the morning, the king went to the lions' den. He yelled out in sadness, "O Daniel, servant of the living God, has your God, whom you serve continually, been able to deliver you from the lions?" (Daniel 6:20).

Then Daniel said to the king "O king, live forever! My God sent his angel and shut the lions' mouths, and they have not harmed me, because I was found blameless before him; and also before you, O king, I have done no harm" (Daniel 6:21–22).

The king was very happy that Daniel was not hurt at all by the lions. Daniel was taken out of the lions' den completely unharmed because he trusted our God. Then the king gathered up all of the jealous men who tricked the king into making a law that would throw Daniel into the lions' den.

The king threw these evil men into the lions' den in the place of Daniel. The lions jumped up and ate the men before they even reached the ground. As a result of God saving Daniel from the lions, King Darius declared to his whole kingdom that Daniel's God (our God) was the one true God and the whole kingdom must love and follow him. God used Daniel being put in a lions' den to convince the whole kingdom that he was the only true God, the one who saved those that trusted in him.

For a while now, the Israelites were living in Babylon because God allowed them to be captured and taken to Babylon by King Nebuchadnezzar because they kept disobeying God. They lived in Babylon for seventy years. After that, God told the kings of Babylon to let them go. At the end of the Old Testament (before Jesus in the Bible), the Israelites (Jews) were once again living in Israel.

Chapter 13

The Book of Jonah

Jonah was an Israelite man. One day, God appeared to Jonah and said, "Arise, go to Nineveh, that great city, and call out against it, for their evil has come up before me" (Jonah 1:2). Nineveh was a huge, pagan city (meaning they did not follow our God). It was located in modern-day Iraq, and it had 120,000 people living in it. God wanted Jonah to go to Nineveh and tell them to repent of their sinful ways. Else God would destroy the city.

Jonah did not want to do this. The city of Nineveh was the capital of the Assyrian Empire, an enemy of the Israelites. Jonah did not want to go there, and he did not want God to save the city. Instead of heading to Nineveh, as God told Jonah to do, he turned around and headed in the completely opposite direction. He found a ship heading to Tarshish and boarded it. Tarshish was west of where Jonah was at; Nineveh was east.

God created a massive storm surrounding the ship that Jonah was on. Everyone on board panicked, and they thought they were going to die. They yelled out to everyone on board to call to the various gods that they worshipped, to see if any would help them in this deadly storm. Things got progressively worse for the people on Jonah's ship. They decided to cast lots to see who might have been responsible for this storm being sent against them. Then lots fell on Jonah.

Jonah revealed that he was a Hebrew and God was sending this storm at them because he was running away from directions God gave him to do. Jonah told them this was all his fault. He said that, if they threw him into the sea and got rid of him, the God of the Hebrews (our God) would stop the storm.

The sailors tried on their own to navigate through the storm, but it was no use, and they were about to die. They concluded that they would have to throw Jonah overboard to save themselves.

> They called out to the Lord, "Oh Lord, let us not perish for this man's life, and lay not on us innocent blood, for you, O Lord, have done as it pleased you." So they picked up Jonah and hurled him into the sea, and the sea ceased from raging. Then the men feared the Lord exceedingly, and they offered a sacrifice to the Lord and made vows. (Jonah 1:14–16)

Jonah now found himself sinking to his death in the ocean. God appointed a great fish to swim up to Jonah and swallow him. Jonah was alive and unharmed in the belly of the great fish for three days and three nights. Jonah was actually very relieved and thankful to be alive and well inside of the huge fish rather than drowning in the ocean, which was what he thought would happen to him. Johan offered up a prayer of thanksgiving to God for saving his life. After these supernatural series of events, Jonah was now willing to obey God's instructions to him.

After three days and nights, God freed Jonah from the belly of the great fish. "And the Lord spoke to the fish, and it vomited Jonah out upon dry land" (Jonah 2:10).

"Then the word of the Lord came to Jonah the second time, saying, 'Arise, go to Nineveh, that great city, and call out against it the message that I tell you'" (Jonah 3:1–2). Jonah went to Nineveh and walked through it, shouting, "Yet forty days, and Nineveh shall be overthrown!" (Jonah 3:4).

Due to the preaching of Jonah, the people of Nineveh believed God, and they repented of their sinful ways. "They called for a fast and put on sackcloth, from the greatest to the least of them" (Jonah 3:5).

News of this reached the king of Nineveh. He ordered the whole kingdom to repent of their evil ways and to call out to God to have mercy on them. "When God saw what they did, how they turned from their evil way, God relented of the disaster that he said he would do to them, and he did not do it" (Jonah 3:10).

Jonah was actually very upset that God saved the people of Nineveh. They were the enemies of Israel, and Jonah did not want God to save them. God responded to Jonah, "Why should I not feel bad for the people in Nineveh? There are one hundred and twenty thousand people in that city who do not know me; therefore, they don't even know that they are doing things that I think are wrong."

Other Books of the Old Testament

Several other books in the Old Testament are not covered in this Bible summary. Please read them on your own. Remember, everything in the Bible is actually the Word of God given to us through human authors.

The Book of Psalms

These are poems and information written by King David. They give us a lot of information about what God is like. They also include many promises about the good things God will do for us if we obey him.

The Book of Ecclesiastes

These are wise stories also written by King Solomon.

The Song of Solomon

Written by King Solomon, it says how a husband and wife should love each other.

The Books of Isaiah, Jeremiah, Lamentations, Ezekiel, Daniel, Hosea, Joel, Amos, Jonah, Micah, Nahum, Habakkuk, Zephaniah, Haggai, Zechariah, and Malachi

There were several prophetic books. In these, God revealed things that would happen in the future. They talked a lot about the coming of the future Messiah, Jesus, who would save the people from their sins and allow people who followed him to get into heaven.

They also gave us other prophetic information about what would happen to both the country of Israel, and the entire world in the future.

Chapter 14

Prophesies about Jesus in the Old Testament

The Old and New Testaments

Up to this point, we have been reading the Old Testament (before Jesus came to earth to save us from our sins). In the Old Testament, people kept sinning, going against the instructions God gave them on how he wanted them to live. God gave them his first plan to save them from their sins, the Law.

If people followed all of God's laws, things would go well for them on earth, and they would get into heaven when they died. However, the people were too weak to follow this, and they kept sinning. God would warn them what would happen to them if they did not stop sinning, and he would punish them if they did not listen to him.

A better plan of God was on the way. He would send his Son, Jesus, to take all of our sins on him and get punished in our place so we would be sinless before God when we died. All we had to do to get this forgiveness of sin is accept that Jesus did this for us and to follow him and what he says.

The Old Testament told the people many times that, in the future, God would send someone to save them. They called this person the Savior, Messiah, or Christ. This person would be God himself, Jesus. The Israelites, or Jews, were waiting for this Savior to come based on the prophesies of the Jewish Bible, which is our Old Testament. Here are some of the predictions from the Old Testament that a savior would be coming.

Prophesies in the Old Testament That Jesus Would Come to Save Us

Genesis 3

Right in the beginning, as soon as Adam and Eve ate the forbidden fruit of the Tree of the Knowledge of Good and Evil, God made some predictions about a Savior. He said to the serpent, which was the devil who had talked Adam and Eve into eating the fruit, "You will be enemies with the offspring of a woman [Jesus, the son of Mary]. He [Jesus] shall bruise your head [defeat the devil], and you shall bruise his heel. [The devil will hurt Jesus by crucifying him, but he will not defeat Jesus]."

God said to Adam, "Because you disobeyed me, the ground will be cursed because of this. When you try to grow food, it will produce thorns." When Jesus was crucified, they made him a crown made out of thorns and put it on his head. This reminded everyone that Jesus was being punished for our sins, which started with Adam and Eve in the garden of Eden.

"If a man has committed a crime punishable by death and he is put to death, and you hang him on a tree, a man hanged on a tree is cursed by God" (Deuteronomy 21:22). Jesus was hung on a tree, "a cross made out of wood," and was cursed by God by taking all of our sins on him and being punished in our place.

The Book of Psalms

King David, who lived seven hundred years before Jesus was born, wrote this book. On many occasions, Jesus guided David on writing about what would happen to him when he came to earth in the future. "The Lord said to me, You are my Son; today I have begotten you. Ask of me, and I will make the nations your heritage, and the ends of the earth your possession" (Psalm 2:7).

God said that Jesus is his only begotten Son. (*Begotten* means to come from; Jesus came from God like a baby comes from its mother.) Also the Bible says that Jesus owns all of the nations and Jesus made everything that exists so he owns everything and does with it what he wants.

> What is man that you are mindful of him, and the son of man that you care for him? Yet you have made him a little lower than the heavenly beings and crowned him with glory and honor. You have given him dominion over the works of your hands; you have put all things under his feet, all sheep and oxen, and also the beasts of the field, the birds of the heavens, and the fish of the sea, whatever passes along the paths of the seas. (Psalm 8:4–8)

When Jesus comes in the future, he calls himself "the Son of Man" all through the New Testament. This psalm by David says that the Son of Man will be ruler of all things.

"My God, My God why have you forsaken me?" Jesus asked this as he was hanging on the cross and God the Father was punishing him in our place for our sins (Psalm 22:1–21).

"I am scorned by mankind and despised by the people. All who see me mock me; they wag their heads; 'He trusts in the Lord; let him deliver him; let him rescue him, for he delights in him'" (Psalm 22:7–8). As Jesus hung on the cross, the people who hung him mocked him and said "If you are really the Son of God, then let God come down and save you from the cross!"

"I am poured out like water, all my bones are out of joint; my heart is like wax; it is melted in my chest, my strength is dried up and my tongue sticks to my jaws; you lay me in the dust of death" (Psalm 22:14–15).

When Jesus was on the cross, many of his bones were pulled out of joint due to the crucifixion. He had no strength, and his tongue was sticking to the inside of his mouth due to extreme thirst.

"For dogs encompass me, a company of evildoers encircles me; they have pierced my hands and my feet—I can count all of my bones—they stare and gloat over me; they divide my garments among them, and for my garments they cast lots" (Psalm 22:16–18).

Jesus was surrounded by evil people who pierced his hands and his feet when they nailed him to the cross. He had a nice coat. The people who took it from him gambled with each other (cast lots) to see who would keep it ("for my garments they cast lots").

"Into your hand I commit my spirit." This was what Jesus would say to God the Father the moment before he died on the cross (Psalm 31:5).

"I looked for pity and there was none, and for comforters, but I found none. They gave me poison for food, and for my thirst they gave me sour wine for drink" (Psalm 69:20). When Jesus was on the cross, they mocked him, harassed him, and gave him sour wine to drink.

Other Old Testament Prophesies about Jesus

> For to us a child is born, to us a son is given; and the government shall be upon his shoulder, and his name shall be called Wonderful Counselor, Mighty God, Everlasting Father, Prince of Peace. Of the increase of his government and of peace there will be no end, on the throne of David and over his kingdom, to establish it and to uphold it with justice and righteousness from this time forth and forevermore. (Isaiah 9:6)

This is telling the Israelites that, in the future, a Savior will be born, and his names describe what he would be like (Prince of Peace). Additionally the book of Revelation states that Jesus will return to earth in the future. When he does, he will rule and govern the entire world from his throne in Jerusalem.

> There shall come forth a shoot from the stump of Jesse, and a branch from his roots shall bear fruit. And the Spirit

of the Lord shall rest upon him, the Spirit of Wisdom and Understanding, the Spirit of Counsel and Might, the Spirit of knowledge and fear of the Lord. And his delight shall be in the fear of the Lord. He shall not judge by what his eyes see, or decide disputes by what his ears hear, but with righteousness he shall judge the poor, and decide with equity for the meek of the earth. (Isaiah 11:1–4)

Jesse was the father of King David. This prophesy says that the Savior (Jesus) would be a descendant of Jesse and King David. It also describes how he will be a judge of the people of the earth and how he will treat the poor people well and fairly.

"Therefore says the Lord God, 'Behold, I am the one who has laid as a foundation in Zion, a stone, a tested stone, a precious cornerstone, of a sure foundation'" (Isaiah 28:16). Jesus would later say, "The stone that the builders have rejected has become the cornerstone." This means that whom the leaders rejected (Jesus) was in fact the most important person.

A voice cries: In the wilderness prepare the way of the Lord; make straight in the desert a highway for our God. Every valley shall be lifted up, and every mountain and hillside be made low; and the uneven ground shall become level, and the rough places a plain. And the glory of the Lord shall be revealed, and all people shall see it together. (Isaiah 40:3)

This was what John the Baptist would actually say in the future to tell the people that the Savior has arrived.

"I gave my back to those who strike, and my cheeks to those who pull out my beard; I hid not my face from disgrace and spitting" (Isiah 51:3). When Jesus would be crucified in the future, they would whip his back with whips, strike him in the face, and pull out parts of his beard. (Remember, Jesus is taking on all of our sins and the rest of the world. He would be punished in our place so we could be declared innocent. So his punishment was very harsh.)

"As many were astonished at you—his appearance was so marred, beyond human recognition, and his body beyond that of human beings" (Isiah 52:13). Jesus would be beaten so badly during the crucifixion events that he could not even be recognized as being a human.

> Surely he has born our griefs and carried our sorrows; He was wounded for our transgressions, crushed for our sins; upon him was the punishment that brought us peace, and by his stripes (wounds) we are healed. The Lord has laid on him the sins of us all. He was oppressed and hurt, yet he did not open his mouth; like a lamb that is led to slaughter, and like a sheep that before its shearers is silent. By oppression and judgment he was taken away, he was cut off out of the land of the living, punished for the sins of the people. They killed him even though he did no violence or anything wrong. (Isaiah 53:4–12)

This describes what Jesus went through to save us so that those who believe in him and accept what he did will be innocent before God.

"In those days and at that time I will cause a righteous Branch to spring up for David, and he shall execute justice and righteousness in the land" (Jeremiah 33:14). Jesus would later be called a Righteous Branch, and he is a descendent of David.

"Strike the shepherd and the sheep will be scattered" (Zechariah 13:7). When the Roman soldiers and Jewish religious leaders grabbed Jesus to be crucified, his twelve apostles became frightened and ran away instead of staying with Jesus.

"But you, O Bethlehem Ephrathah, who are too little to be among the clans of Judah, from you shall come forth for me one who is to be ruler of Israel, whose coming forth is from days of old, from ancient days" (Micah 5:2). This predicts that Jesus will be born in Bethlehem.

Malachi is the last prophet before Jesus. After Malachi's writing (the book of Malachi), there were no messages from God to the people until Jesus would come four hundred years later.

"Behold, I send my messenger, and he will prepare the way for me. And the Lord whom you seek will suddenly come to his temple; and the messenger of the covenant in whom you delight, behold, he is coming, says the Lord of hosts" (Malachi 2:1). God would send John the Baptist, who was Jesus's cousin, to tell all of Israel that their Savior was here and would be showing himself soon.

"Behold, I will send you Elijah the prophet before the great and awesome day of the Lord comes. And he will turn the hearts of the fathers to their children and the hearts of children to their fathers" (Malachi 4:1). This is a final prediction that God will send John the Baptist, who will have the spirit of Elijah, to prepare the way for the coming of God to earth, Jesus. Or this may be referring to God actually sending Elijah back as one of the two witnesses in the book of Revelation to prepare the way for Jesus's second coming.

Chapter 15

The New Testament

The Early Life of Jesus

The New Testament is the second half of the Bible. It is all about Jesus. It starts off with the birth of Jesus and then tells about his whole life and what happened after he rose from the dead and went back to heaven. The Gospels are the four books in the Bible that were written about Jesus's life on earth—Matthew, Mark, Luke, and John. I will combine parts from the four gospel books to tell the story of Jesus.

Remember, although Jesus did many great things here on earth, his main reason for coming here was to take all of our sins on him and get punished in our place (crucified). We now don't have to get punished by God because Jesus took care of our sins. We are now seen as innocent of sin by God, and we will be allowed into heaven when we die *if we accept Jesus as our God and follow him in our lives.*

> In the beginning was the Word, and the Word was with God, and the Word was God (Jesus is the Word of God). He was in the beginning with God. All things were made through him, and without him was not anything made that was made (Jesus made the entire universe before he came down to earth as a man). In him was life, and the life was the light of men. The light shines in the darkness, and the darkness has not overcome it. (John 1:1–5)

Jesus is the light of the world.

"There was a man sent from God, whose name was John (Jesus's cousin, John the Baptist). He came as a witness, to bear witness about the light, that all might believe through him. John was not the light, but came to bear witness about the light" (John 1:6–8).

> The true light, which enlightens everyone, was coming into the world. He was in the world, and the world was made through him, yet the world did not know him. He came to his own, and his own people did not receive him. But to all who did receive him, who believed in his name, he gave the right to become children of God, who were born, not of blood nor of the will of the flesh nor of the will of man, but of God. (John 1:9–13)

If we accept that Jesus died to pay for our sins, we will become children of God and go to heaven when we die.

> And the Word became flesh and lived among us, we have seen his glory, glory as of the only Son from the Father, full of grace and truth. (Jesus became a man who came to earth and lived with the people of Israel for thirty-three years. John bore witness about him and cried out, "This is the one of whom I said 'He who comes after me ranks before me, because he was before me.'") And from his fullness we have all received grace upon grace. (The word *grace* means you were given something very good that you do not deserve. This means that God forgives our sins through Jesus because he loves us, even though we do not deserve it.) For the law was given through Moses (the Old Testament); grace and truth came through Jesus Christ. (In the Old Testament, the people had to follow all of God's laws perfectly to be sinless to God. Jesus made it so, if we follow him, God forgives all of our sins because Jesus was punished in our place.) No one has ever seen God; the

only God, who is at the Father's side, he has made him
known. (John 1:14–18)

Matthew 1:1–17 and Luke 3:23–38 show how Jesus came from a family
whose ancestors included Adam, Seth, Enoch, Noah, Abraham, Isaac,
Jacob, Judah, Ruth, Jesse, King David, King Solomon, and eventually
Joseph, the husband of Mary, who was Jesus's mother.

Remember, because Abraham and David trusted God, God promised that
their children would form a great nation and people. What could be greater
that one of your great-great-great great grandsons being Jesus, who is God
that came to save all of us from our sins!

The Birth of John the Baptist

The birth of Jesus is given in the most detail in the book of Luke, one
of the Gospels that was written about when Jesus came to earth. Jesus's
mother, Mary, was related to a woman named Elizabeth. Elizabeth was
older and did not have any children, and she prayed to God that he would
give her a child.

One day, an angel of God came to her husband, Zechariah. He told
Zechariah that God heard their prayers and would make his wife,
Elizabeth, pregnant with a son. He would be named John. John would be
great before God, and he would be filled with the Holy Spirit. He would
turn many of the children of Israel to the Lord their God, and he would
go before God in the spirit and power of Elijah to turn the hearts of the
fathers to the children and the disobedient to the wisdom of the just, all
so he could get the people ready for the coming of Jesus.

Prophets in the Old Testament predicted that John the Baptist would come
to tell the people that their Savior, Jesus, had arrived. For example, four
hundred years earlier, the prophet Malachi sent a message from God to the
Israelites, "Behold, I send my messenger, and he will prepare the way for
me. I will send you Elijah the prophet before the great and awesome day
of the Lord comes. And he will turn the hearts of fathers to their children,
and the hearts of children to their fathers."

The Birth of Jesus

God sent the angel Gabriel to a young woman named Mary who lived in a small town in Israel Galilee named Nazareth. Mary was engaged to marry a man named Joseph. The angel Gabriel said to Mary that God was pleased with her. God would make her pregnant with a son, and she would name him Jesus.

"He will be great and will be called the Son of the Most High. And the Lord God will give to him the throne of his ancestor, King David, and he will rule over the house of Jacob forever, and there will be no end to his kingdom" (Luke 1:32–33).

Mary told the angel Gabriel that she would do whatever God asked her to do. So Mary became pregnant with Jesus. During this time, she visited Elizabeth, who was pregnant with a boy that would be John the Baptist, the man that God would send to announce the coming of the Savior, Jesus.

When Elizabeth saw Mary, John the Baptist leaped for joy in Elizabeth's womb. Elizabeth said to Mary, "Blessed are you among women, and blessed is the fruit of your womb!" This would later become part of the prayer "Hail Mary."

During this time in history, Israel, along with much of Europe, Africa, and Asia, had been conquered by the Romans and was part of the Roman Empire. At this time, Caesar Augustus, the emperor of the Roman Empire, declared that a census must be taken in everyone's hometown to see how many people were living in each area of the Roman Empire.

Mary, the woman who was pregnant with Jesus, went with her husband, Joseph, to Bethlehem for the census. Joseph had to get registered in Bethlehem because he was a descendant of King David, who was also from Bethlehem. You will see shortly how God caused this census to happen to cause Jesus to be born in Bethlehem instead of Nazareth, to protect Jesus from those who would want to kill him.

"And while they were there, the time came for Mary to give birth. And she gave birth to her firstborn son, and named him Jesus, and wrapped him in swaddling clothes and laid him in a manger, because there was no place for them in the inn" (Luke 2:6–7).

There was a prophesy that a special star would rise in the sky when the Savior was born, and this happened. Wise men from the East saw this star and came to Jerusalem looking for the Savior. They came to the king of Israel, King Herod, in the city of Jerusalem.

They said to King Herod, "We saw his star when it rose, and we have come to worship him."

This bothered King Herod. He did not want anyone to be king except him. He asked the priests, "Where does the Jewish Bible say the Savior would be born?"

In the book of Micah, it said that he would be born in Bethlehem. King Herod told the wise men to go to Bethlehem and find the baby that was born who would be the Savior. Then they were to come back and tell King Herod where he was at so he could also go and worship him.

They followed the star in the sky until they came to a manger right beneath it, where Jesus, Mary, and Joseph were. They worshipped the baby Jesus and gave him gifts. On the way back, God came to them in a dream and told them not to go back to King Herod and tell him where Jesus was because he wanted to kill Jesus. So they went home another way.

After the wise men left Jesus, an angel came to Joseph in a dream. He told Joseph to take Jesus and Mary to Egypt and hide there because King Herod would try to kill Jesus because he was jealous of him. So Joseph took Jesus and Mary to Egypt.

When King Herod realized that the wise men were not coming back to tell him where Jesus was, he became furious. King Herod did not know which child was Jesus. Therefore, he sent in the army to kill *all* of the boys in Bethlehem age two and under, in an attempt to get rid of Jesus.

This is another example of a power-hungry king doing evil things to hold on to his power. Eventually, King Herod died, and Jesus, Mary, and Joseph returned to Nazareth. No one was looking for him in Nazareth because they thought he would be living in Bethlehem. Jesus was only born in Bethlehem when Joseph and Mary had to go there for the census. This helped protect Jesus because no one was looking for him in Nazareth (Matthew 2).

The Boy Jesus in the Temple

Every year, Jesus, Mary, and Joseph went to the city of Jerusalem with a big group of other people to celebrate the Passover feast. One year when Jesus was twelve, he stayed behind in Jerusalem after his parents headed back to Nazareth. They eventually realized Jesus was not with the group, so they returned to Jerusalem to look for him.

It took them three days to find him. He was in the temple, which was their church. He was talking with the priests, and everyone who heard him was amazed at how much he knew about everything.

His parents asked him why he would get them so upset by staying behind after they left to return home.

Jesus said, "Why were you looking for me? Did you not know that I must be in my Father's house?" (Luke 2:49).

Chapter 16

Jesus Begins His Ministry

Nothing is written in the Bible about Jesus when he was between the ages of twelve to thirty. Although he was 100 percent God and 100 percent man, it is assumed that he lived the life of a regular person during this time. It is believed that he was a carpenter, like his stepfather, Joseph. Sometime during the time between when Jesus was twelve and thirty, his stepfather, Joseph, died, but no details were given about that.

At age thirty, Jesus began a three-year period that ended with him taking all of our sins on him and dying on the cross. During this time, he stopped being a carpenter. He went out and told all of Israel that he was the Savior that they had been told about in the Jewish Bible that would come to save them. He did countless spectacular miracles to prove beyond a doubt that he was God. He also taught the people all about God. This three-year period is called Jesus's ministry.

At the time when Jesus was thirty, John the Baptist was the biggest preacher in the land. He would stand out in public and talk about God. He told the people to stop sinning and turn back to following God. He also told him that the Savior, or Messiah, would be coming very soon to save the people from their sins.

The Old Testament states in many places that a man would come to announce the coming of the Savior, and that man was John the Baptist.

One day, John the Baptist was baptizing people, and Jesus walked up to him. When John saw Jesus, he said,

> Behold, the Lamb of God, who takes away the sin of the world! This is he of whom I said "After me comes a man who ranks before me, because he was before me." I myself did not know him, but for this purpose I came baptizing with water, that he might be revealed to Israel. God, who sent me, showed me who he is. And I have seen and born witness that this is the Son of God. (John 1:29–34)

So John the Baptist, who everybody listened to, told Israel that Jesus was the Son of God who came here to take away the sins of the world. Jesus asked John to baptize him, which John was honored to do.

When John the Baptist baptized Jesus in front of the crowd, the heavens were opened, and the Holy Spirit came down on Jesus in the form of a dove. The voice of God came from heaven. "You are my beloved Son; with you I am well pleased" (Matthew 3:17).

The Calling of the Disciples

The first thing that Jesus did when he began his ministry was to gather disciples. People who followed Jesus were called his disciples. There twelve disciples were the closest to Jesus and followed him wherever he went. These closest disciples were called the twelve apostles. The twelve apostles were Peter, James, John, Andrew, Philip, Bartholomew, Matthew, Thomas, a second James, Thaddaeus, Simon, and Judas. Out of the twelve apostles, Jesus was closest to three: James; John, who was Jesus's best friend; and Peter.

The Wedding at Cana

Jesus was at a wedding with his mother, Mary, and his disciples. They ran out of wine at the wedding. Mary told Jesus to do something to help. Jesus said no because it was not time for him yet to start doing miracles. She insisted that he help. Jesus told the waiters to fill six big jars with water.

Jesus turned the water into wine. It was the best wine that they had ever tasted. This was the first miracle that Jesus ever did.

The Temptation of Jesus

The Holy Spirit led Jesus into the wilderness so the devil could tempt him. This was done to see if Jesus were holy and worthy to pay for the sins for all of us. He fasted (did not eat food) for forty days and nights, and he was hungry.

At that time, the devil came to tempt him to sin and said, "If you are the Son of God, command these stones to become loaves of bread" (Matthew 4:3).

God the Father told Jesus to fast (not eat), and the devil tried to get Jesus to disobey God the Father. Jesus answered, "It is written, man shall not live by bread alone, but by every word that comes from the mouth of God" (Matthew 4:4).

Then the devil took Jesus to the top of the Jewish temple and said, "If you are the Son of God, throw yourself down, for it is written 'He will command his angels concerning you, and in their hands they will catch you so your foot will not strike against a stone'"(Matthew 4:5–6).

Jesus said to the devil, "Again it is written, 'You shall not put the Lord your God to the test'" (Matthew 4:7).

Next, the devil took Jesus to a very high mountain and showed him all of the kingdoms of the world and their glory. And he said to Jesus, "All of these I will give to you if you will fall down and worship me."

Then Jesus said to him,

> Be gone Satan! For it is written, "You shall worship the Lord your God and him only shall you serve." And when the devil had ended every temptation for Jesus to sin, he left him, waiting for another opportunity to destroy

Jesus. Then angels came to Jesus and took care of him. (Matthew 4:8–11)

The Miracles of Jesus

Jesus performed many, many miracles for the people of Israel. He did this for two main reasons:

1. He loved the people, and in many of his miracles, he healed them from illnesses and problems that they had.
2. He did these miracles so that everyone would know without a doubt that he was God.

No man could do any of the miracles that Jesus did. Only God could do them. Here are some of the many miracles Jesus performed.

- A man had leprosy, a terrible skin disease. He came to Jesus and said, "Lord, if you will, you can make me healed." Jesus said, "I will; be healed." Immediately the man's leprosy was healed.
- One day a centurion, a Roman soldier, came up to Jesus. He told Jesus that a servant of his was paralyzed back at home and was suffering greatly. He asked Jesus if he could heal him. Jesus said, "I will come and heal him" (Matthew 8:7). The centurion said that he was not worthy to have Jesus enter his home, but if Jesus just said the word, he knew that his servant would be healed. He said that he knew that Jesus had authority over everything and had the power to heal his servant from wherever he was at. Jesus said that he had never come across anyone in Israel that had faith in him as strong as this centurion. "And to the centurion Jesus said, 'Go; let it be done for you as you have believed.' And the servant was healed at that very moment" (Matthew 8:13).
- Some people brought a paralyzed man to Jesus to be healed. When Jesus saw their faith, he said, "Take heart, my son; your sins are forgiven" (Matthew 9:2). The man stood up and went home. When the crowds saw it, they were afraid, and they glorified God, who had given such authority to Jesus.

- Jesus was talking to a group of people. A man came up to him and said, "My daughter has just died, but come and lay your hand on her and she will live" (Matthew 9:18). Jesus went to the man's house. He held the hand of the little girl, and she came back to life. A report of this went through all that town.

- When Jesus was leaving the neighborhood of the girl he brought back to life, two blind men followed him, yelling, "Have mercy on us, Son of David!" (Matthew 9:27). He touched their eyes, and they could see.

- As the blind men were walking away, a demon-possessed man who could not speak because of it was brought to Jesus. Jesus cast the demon out, and the man spoke. The Pharisees (priests) said, "He casts out demons because he is a demon." (The Pharisees were jealous that Jesus had special powers that they did not have and he was getting a lot of attention. The Pharisees were the ones who would crucify Jesus soon.)

- One time, Jesus was speaking to a crowd of several thousand. There was no food there, and people were starting to get hungry. The apostles only had five loaves of bread and two fish. Jesus looked up to heaven and blessed it, and God multiplied it so there was enough food to feed the several thousand people. They had twelve baskets of food left over. Jesus did the exact same thing a little bit later when the crowd he was speaking to was hungry and there was no food.

- After they fed the people, Jesus sent the disciples away in a boat, and he went up a mountain to pray. Later in the night, Jesus walked out on the water toward the apostles who were in the boat. They thought it was a ghost, and they were afraid. He said to them, "Take heart; it is I. Do not be afraid." When Peter saw him, he said, "Lord, if it is you, command me to come to you on the water." Jesus said, "Come." Peter got out of the boat and walked on the water toward Jesus. He then noticed the wind, became afraid, and started to sink. He yelled, "Lord, save me!" Jesus grabbed him and said, "O you of little faith, why did you doubt?" The apostles began to worship him, saying, "Truly you are the Son of God" (Matthew 14:27–33).

- People brought a man to Jesus who was deaf and also unable to speak. They begged Jesus to heal him. Jesus put his fingers into the man's ears, touched the man's tongue, and said, "Be opened." He immediately could hear and speak. The crowd was amazed and said, "Jesus has done all things well. He even makes the deaf hear and the mute speak" (Mark 7:32–37).
- Jesus went on from here and sat down on a mountain. People were brought to him who were blind or crippled or could not speak, along with those that had other diseases and illnesses. And Jesus healed them all.

There were several people who did not believe in God, and they did not trust him. Since they did not want God's help, God did not protect them, and evil spirits entered the people, possessed them, and made them sick and very unhappy. Many of these people were brought to Jesus to be healed. Jesus told the evil spirits they had to leave each person and never come back. Jesus has power over everything, even demons and devils, so they had to listen to him. The evil spirits left the people, and they were well. The people who saw this were amazed.

Jesus Calms a Storm

One day, Jesus got into a boat with his disciples and he said to them "Let us go across to the other side of the lake." So they set out, and as they sailed, Jesus fell asleep. A windstorm came down on the lake, and the boat was filling with water and they were in danger. Then disciples woke Jesus, saying "Master, Master, we are perishing!" Jesus awoke and rebuked the wind and the waves and they ceased, and there was a calm. He said to them "Where is your faith?" And they were afraid and they marveled, saying to one another, "Who then is this, that he commands even the winds and water, and they obey him?" (Luke 8:22–25)

The Transfiguration

> One day, Jesus took the 3 apostles he was closest to; Peter,
> James, and John with him to a mountain top. There, Jesus
> transfigured, or turned in to what he looks like when he
> is in heaven. His face glowed like the sun, and his clothes
> became white as light. Then Moses and Elijah came down
> from heaven and was talking with Jesus. All of a sudden,
> a bright cloud hovered over all of them. God the Father
> spoke out of this cloud and said "This is my beloved Son,
> with whom I am well pleased; listen to him." (Matthew
> 17:6–7)

When the apostles heard this, they fell on their face and were terrified.
Jesus came and touched them, saying, "Rise and have no fear" (Matthew
17:7). When they lifted up their eyes, they saw no one but Jesus with them.

Jesus Raises Lazarus from the Dead

There was a man named Lazarus, who was a friend of Jesus. Lazarus' sisters
were named Martha and Mary, and they were also friends of Jesus. One
day, Lazarus became very sick. Martha and Mary sent a message to Jesus,
letting him know that his friend Lazarus was sick.

Jesus responded, "This Illness does not lead to death. It is for the Glory
of God, so that the Son of God may be glorified through it" (John 11:4).

Jesus loved Martha, Mary, and Lazarus. When he heard Lazarus was sick,
he purposely waited two days until he went to see Lazarus. After two days,
Jesus said to his disciples, "Let us go to Judea. Our friend Lazarus has fallen
asleep, but I go to awaken him" (John 11:11).

The disciples said, if he fell asleep, that was good because it would help
Lazarus get better. They did not understand that he actually died.

Jesus then said to them, "Lazarus has died, and for your sake I am glad
that I was not there, so that you may believe. But let us go to him" (John

11:14). (If he were just sick and Jesus made him better, that would be a minor miracle. If Jesus brought him back from the dead, that would be a *major* miracle and lead witnesses to this to believe Jesus was God.)

When Jesus arrived, Lazarus had already been dead and buried in a tomb for four days. Martha ran out to Jesus when he arrived. She said, "Lord, it you had been here, my brother would not have died. But even now I know that whatever you ask from God, God will give you" (John 11:21–22).

Jesus said to Martha, "I am the resurrection and the life. Whoever believes in me, though he die, yet shall he live, and everyone who lives and believes in me shall never die. Do you believe this?"

Martha said, "Yes Lord; I believe that you are the Christ, the Son of God, who is coming into the world" (John 11:25–27).

Mary came out of the house along with a crowd of people to meet Jesus. Mary said to Jesus, "Lord, if you had been here, my brother would not have died" (John 11:32).

Everyone was crying. Jesus was greatly moved by this, and he cried along with his friends. Jesus and the crowd went to the tomb where Lazarus had been buried for four days. It was a cave, with a stone placed over the covering. Jesus told them to take away the stone. They were afraid of the smell that would come out since Lazarus had been dead for four days.

Jesus said, "Did I not tell you that, if you believed, you would see the glory of God?" Jesus said, "Father, I thank you that you have heard me. I knew that you always hear me, but I said this on account of the people standing around that that they may believe that you sent me." Then Jesus said with a loud voice, "Lazarus, come out" (John 11:40–43).

Lazarus, who was dead for four days, came out. His hands and feet were bound with linen strips, and his face was wrapped with a cloth. Jesus told the people to untie him and let Lazarus go. Many of the witnesses of this came to believe that Jesus was the Christ.

Chapter 17

The Teachings of Jesus

Jesus performed all of the miracles stated above, along with additional others that were not listed here, to prove without a doubt that he was God. Another thing that Jesus did during his three-year ministry was that he taught the people about himself as God the Savior, God the Father, and heaven, among other things. These are some but not all of his teachings. To learn about all of Jesus's teachings, please read the Gospels of Matthew, Mark, Luke, and John in the Bible.

Jesus said that the way to love him is to read to the Bible and do what it says in your life. Jesus said, "Whoever has my commandments and keeps them, he is it who loves me. And he who loves me will be loved by my Father, and I will love him and manifest myself to him" (John 14:21).

Jesus said,

> If you love me, you will keep my commandments. And I will ask the Father, and he will give you another Helper, to be with you forever, even the Spirit if truth, whom the world cannot receive, because it neither sees him or knows him. You know him, for he dwells with you and will be in you. (John 14:15–17)

Jesus said, "If anyone loves me, he will keep my word, and my Father will love him, and we will come to him and make our home with him" (John 14:23).

> Whatever we ask we receive from God, because we keep his commandments and do what pleases him. And this is his commandment, that we believe in the name of his Son Jesus Christ and love one another, just as he commanded us. Whoever keeps his commandments abides in God, and God abides in him. And by this we know that he abides in us, by the Spirit whom he has given us. (1 John 3:22–24)

Jesus said, "You are my friends if you do what I command you. No longer do I call you servants, for the servant does not know what the master is doing, but I have called you friends, for all that I have heard from my Father I have made known to you" (John 15:14–15).

Whoever Does the Will of God Will Be a Family Member of Jesus

> While Jesus was still speaking to the people, behold, his mother and his brothers stood outside, asking to speak to him. But he replied to the man who told him, "Who is my mother, and who are my brothers?" And stretching out his hand to his disciples, he said "Here are my mother and my brothers! *For whoever does the will of my Father in heaven is my brother and sister and mother.*" (Matthew 12:46–50)

The Beatitudes

Jesus went up on a mountain and taught the following to the crowd, which is called the *beatitudes*. He basically said that God will help people who love and put their trust in him and have a good heart.

> Blessed are the poor in spirit for theirs is the kingdom of heaven. Blessed are those who mourn, for they shall be comforted. Blessed are the meek, for they shall inherit

the earth. Blessed are those who hunger and thirst for righteousness, for they shall be satisfied. Blessed are the merciful, for they shall receive mercy. Blessed are the pure in heart, for they shall see God. Blessed are the peacemakers, for they shall be called sons of God. Blessed are those who are persecuted for righteousness sake, for theirs is the kingdom of heaven. Blessed are you when others criticize you and persecute you and utter all kinds of evil against you falsely on my account. Rejoice and be glad, for your reward is great in heaven, because they persecuted the prophets who were before you. (Matthew 5:3–12)

Salt and Light

Jesus said that Christians are to be good, consistent examples of followers of Christ to the rest of the world. Jesus said,

You are the salt of the earth. But if salt has lost its taste, how shall its saltiness to be restored? It is no longer good for anything except to be thrown out and trampled under people's feet. You are the light of the world. A city set on a hill cannot be hidden. Nor do people light a lamp and put it under a basket, but on a stand, and it gives light to all in the house. In the same way, let your light shine before others, so that they may see your good works and give glory to your father who is in heaven. (Matthew 5:13–16)

Jesus Came to Fulfill the Law

Jesus said, "Do not think I came to abolish the Law or the Prophets; I have not come to abolish them, but to fulfill them" (Matthew 5:17–20).

Do Not Have Anger in Your Hearts and Make Peace with Each Other

Jesus said that, although the Law says you will be liable to judgement if you murder, having anger in your heart toward anyone is wrong and a sin.

If you have anything against anyone in your heart or you know of another person who has something against you, stop what you are doing, go to that person, and attempt to make peace with him or her.

Avoid Lust

Jesus said that adultery is a sin. However, if you have lustful intents in your heart, that is also sinning. Do whatever you can do to avoid lustful thoughts to entice you. Do whatever you have to do to avoid the temptations that cause these lustful thoughts.

Seek Mercy, Not Revenge

Jesus said you must not try to get revenge against others that you believe have done wrong by you. Additionally, you should be very generous in your giving help to others who ask for it or are in need of it.

Love Your Enemies

Jesus said,

> You have heard that it was said "You shall love your neighbor and hate your enemy." But I say to you, love your enemies and pray for those that persecute you, so that you may be the sons of your Father who is in heaven. For he makes the sun rise on the evil and the good, and sends rain on the just and the unjust. For if you love those that love you, what reward do you have? Do not even the tax collectors do the same? And if you greet only your brothers, what more are you doing than others? Do not even the gentiles do the same? You therefore must be perfect, as your heavenly Father is perfect. (Matthew 5:43)

Be Generous to Others, But Don't Do It to Show Off

Jesus said,

Beware of practicing your righteousness before other people *in order to be seen by them,* for then you will have no reward from your father who is in heaven. Thus, when you give to the needy, sound no trumpet before you, as the hypocrites do in the synagogues and in the streets, that they may be praised by others. Truly I say to you, they have received their reward (the praise they got from others). But when you give to the needy, do not let your left hand know what your right hand is doing, so that your giving may be in secret. And your Father who sees in secret will reward you. (Matthew 6:1–4)

Jesus Gives Us the Lord's Prayer

Jesus said that, when you pray, do not do it in a way to show off to be noticed by others. Pray in a personal way between you and God your Father. Also when you pray, do not use a bunch of long, empty phrases. God does not care how many words you use when you pray. Jesus said,

Pray then like this: Our Father in heaven, Hallowed be your name. Your kingdom come, Your will be done, On earth as it is in heaven. Give us this day our daily bread, And forgive us our debts, As we have also forgiven our debtors. And lead us not into temptation, But deliver us from evil. (Matthew 6:9–13)

Jesus then next said, "For if you forgive others their trespasses, your heavenly Father will also forgive you, but if you do not forgive others their trespasses, neither will your Father forgive Your trespasses" (Matthew 6:14–15).

Do Good Things to Lay Up Treasures for Yourself in Heaven Instead of Treasures on Earth

Jesus said,

Do not lay up for yourselves treasures on earth, where moth and rust destroy and where thieves break in and steal, but lay up for yourselves treasures in heaven, where neither moth nor rust destroys and where thieves do not break in and steal. For where your treasure is, your heart will be also. (Matthew 6:19–23)

Do Not Worry about Anything; If You Follow God, He Will Take Care of You

Jesus said to not worry about your life, what you eat or drink, or what you will wear. The animals and plants do not worry about these things, and God your Father takes care of all of them. You are much more valuable to him than those are.

Can worrying about things help you in any way? God is your Father, and he knows you need these things. He will supply them for you. Instead of worrying about all of the things of the world, seek out the kingdom of God and his righteousness. When you do, all of the worldly things will additionally be given to you. Additionally, do not worry about what will happen in the future. Focus on what you need to do today, and the future will take care of itself.

Don't Judge Other People; Instead Focus on Fixing Your Own Flaws So You Can Be a Better Person

Jesus said,

> Judge not, that you be not judged. For with the judgment you pronounce you will be judged, and with the measure you use it will be measured to you. Why do you see that speck in your brother's eye, but you do not notice the log that is in your own eye? Or how can you say to your brother "Let me take the speck out of your eye," when there is a log in your own eye? You hypocrite, first take the log out of your own eye, and then you will see clearly to take the speck out of your brother's eye. (Matthew 7:1–5)

If You Are a Child of God, He Will Give You Good Things That Are Aligned with His Will If You Ask Him

Jesus said,

> Ask, and it will be given to you; seek, and you will find; knock, and it will be open to you. For everyone who asks receives, and the one who seeks finds, and the one who knocks it will be opened. Or which one of you, if his son asks him for bread, will give him a stone? Or if he asks for a fish, will give him a serpent? If you then, who are evil, know how to give good gifts to *your children*, how much more will your Father who is in heaven give good things and the *Holy Spirit* to those who ask him!" (Matthew 7:7–11; Luke 11:9–13)

The Golden Rule

Jesus said, "So whatever you wish that others would do to you, do also to them, for this is the Law and the Prophets" (Matthew 7:12).

Reading the Bible and Doing What It Says Will Shelter You Throughout Your Life

Jesus said,

> Everyone who *hears these words of mine and does them* will be like a wise man who built his house on the rock. And the rain fell, and the floods came, and the winds blew and beat on that house, but it did not fall, because it had been founded on the rock. And everyone who hears these words of mine *and does not do them* will be like a foolish man who built his house on the sand. And then rain fell, and the floods came, and the winds blew and beat against that house, and it fell, and great was the fall of it. (Matthew 7:24–27)

Jesus Came for Those Who Want Him and Know They Need Him

Jesus saw a man, a tax collector named Matthew. (It was a bad thing to be in those days because they were often corrupt.) Jesus said to him, "Follow me," and Matthew rose and followed Jesus. Jesus was later with Matthew in a big house with a lot of guests. Many tax collectors and sinners were hanging out with Jesus and his disciples because they knew they were sinners and needed Jesus to save them.

> When the Pharisees (priests) saw this, they said to Jesus's disciples, "Why does your teacher eat with tax collectors and sinners?" Jesus heard this and said to them "Those who are well do not need a doctor, but those who are sick do. Go and learn what this means, 'I desire mercy, not sacrifice.' For I came not to call the righteous, but sinners." (The priests thought they were holy and sinless and did not need Jesus, even though they needed him *the most*.) (Matthew 9:9–13)

If You Come to Jesus, He Will Give You Rest and Guidance

Jesus said, "Come to me, all who labor and are heavy laden, and I will give you rest. Take my yoke upon you, and learn from me, for I am gentle and lowly in heart, and you will find rest for your souls. For my yoke is easy, and my burden is light" (Matthew 11:28–30).

He who hears God's Word, understands it, and does it will be productive for God.

The Parable of the Sower

Jesus told the crowds,

> A sower went out to sow. And as he sowed, some seeds fell along the path, and the birds came and devoured them. Other seeds fell on rocky ground, where they did not have much soil, and immediately they sprang up, since

they had no depth of soil, but when the sun rose they were scorched. And since they had to root, they withered away. Other seeds fell among thorns, and the thorns grew up and choked them. Other seeds fell on good soil and produced grain, some a hundredfold, some sixty, some thirty. He who has ears, let him hear. (Matthew 13:3–8)

The disciples asked Jesus to explain the parable of the sower to them, and Jesus told them,

When anyone hears the word of the kingdom and does not understand it, the evil one comes and snatches away what has been sown in his heart. This is what was sown along the path. As for what was sown on rocky ground, this is the one who hears the word and immediately receives it with joy, yet he has no root in himself, but endures for a while, and when tribulation or persecution arises on account of the word, immediately he falls away. As for what was sown among thorns, this is the one who hears the word, but the cares of the world and the deceitfulness of riches choke the word, and it proves unfruitful. As for what was sown on good soil, this is the one who hears the word and understands it. He indeed bears fruit and yields, in one case a hundredfold, in another sixty, and in another thirty. (Matthew 13:19–23)

Parables about Heaven

Jesus said, "The kingdom of heaven is like treasure hidden in a field, which a man found and covered up. Then in his joy he goes and sells all that he has and buys that field" (Matthew 13:44).

Jesus said, "Again, the kingdom of heaven is like a merchant in search of great pearls, who finding one pearl of great value, went and sold all he had and bought it" (Matthew 13:45–46).

Follow Jesus and Save Your Soul

Jesus told his disciples,

> If anyone would come after me, let him deny himself and take up his cross and follow me. For whoever would save his life would lose it, but whoever loses his life for my sake will find it. For what will it profit a man if he gains the whole world and forfeits his soul? Or what shall a man give in return for his soul? For the Son of Man is going to come with his angels in the glory of his Father, and then he will repay each person according to what he has done. (Matthew 16:24–27)

Being Humble, Like a Child, Makes One Great in Heaven

The disciples asked Jesus, "Who is the greatest in the kingdom of heaven?" Jesus grabbed a child and said, "Truly I say to you, unless you turn and become like children, you will never enter the kingdom of heaven. *Whoever humbles himself like this is the greatest in the kingdom of heaven*" (Matthew 18:1–6).

Do Not Cause Others to Sin, Especially Children

Jesus said, "Whoever receives one such child in my name receives me, but whoever causes one of these little ones who believe in me to sin, it would be better for him to have a great millstone fastened around his neck and to be drowned in the depth of the sea" (Matthew 18:5–6).

The Parable of the Unforgiving Servant

The following parable demonstrates that, since Jesus forgives *all* of our sins when we follow him, should we not be grateful and follow his example and forgive the *few* sins others have committed against us?

> Then Peter came up and said to Jesus, "Lord, how often will my brother sin against me, and I forgive him? As

many as seven times?" Jesus said to him "I do not say to you seven times, but seventy times seven." Therefore the kingdom of heaven may be compared to a king who wished to settle accounts with his servants. When he began to settle, one was brought to him and owed ten thousand talents (a vast amount of money). And since he could not pay, his master ordered him to be sold, with his wife and his children and all that he had, and payment to be made. So the servant fell on his knees, imploring him, "Have patience with me, and I will pay you everything." *And out of pity for him, the master of that servant released him and forgave him the debt.* But when the same servant went out, he found one of his fellow servants who owed him a hundred denarii (a small amount of money), and seizing him, he began to choke him, saying, "Pay what you owe." So his fellow servant fell down and pleaded with him, "Have patience with me, and I will pay you." He refused and went and put him in prison until he should pay the debt. When his fellow servants saw what had taken place, they were greatly distressed, and they went and reported to their master all that had taken place. Then his master summoned him and said to him, "You wicked servant! I forgave you all that debt because you pleaded with me. And should you not have had mercy on your fellow servant, as I had mercy on you?" And in anger his master delivered him to the jailers, until he should pay all his debt. So also my heavenly Father will do to every one of you, if you do not forgive your brother from your heart. (Matthew 18:21–35)

Parable of the Laborers in the Vineyard

God is generous in saving anyone who decides to follow him, no matter when he or she does it in his or her lifetime. Jesus said,

For the kingdom of heaven is like a master of a house who went out early in the morning to hire laborers for his vineyard. After agreeing with the laborers for a denarius a day, he sent them into the vineyard. And going out about the third hour he saw others standing idle in the marketplace, and to them he said "You go into the vineyard too, and whatever is right I will give you." So they went. Going out again about the sixth hour and the ninth hour, he did the same. And about the eleventh hour he went out and found others standing. And he said to them, "Why do you stand here idle all day?" They said to him, "Because no one has hired us." He said to them, "You go into the vineyard too." And when evening came, the owner of the vineyard said to his foreman, "Call the laborers and pay them their wages, beginning with the last, up to the first." And when those hired about the eleventh hour came, each received a denarius. Now when those hired first came, they thought they would receive more, but each of them also received a denarius. And on receiving it they grumbled at the master of the house, saying "These last worked only one hour, and you have made them equal to us who have borne the burden of the day and the scorching heat." But he replied to one of them, "Friend, I am doing you no wrong. Did you not agree with me for a denarius? Take what belongs to you and go. *I choose to give to this last worker as I give to you. Am I not allowed to do what I choose with what belongs to me? Or do you begrudge my generosity?*" So the last will be first, and the first will be last. (Matthew 20:1–16)

Repentance

Jesus posed a question to the people.

A man had two sons. He went to the first and said "Son, go and work in the vineyard today." The son answered "I will not," but afterward he changed his mind and went and worked. The father went to the second son and said the same. The son answered "I will go dad," but he did not go. Which one did the will of his father? The crowd said "The first." Jesus said to the crowd that many of them will not get into heaven because even though Jesus was telling them that they need to believe in him and follow him, many were not changing their minds and doing this. Or, they were just following Jesus with their words, but not with their actions.

All of Heaven Rejoices When a Sinner Comes to Jesus and Is Saved

Jesus said,

> What man of you, having a hundred sheep, if he has lost one of them, does not leave the ninety-nine in the open country, and go after the one that is lost, until he finds it? And when he has found it, he lays it on his shoulders, rejoicing. And when he comes home, he calls together his friends and his neighbors, saying to them, "Rejoice with me, for I have found my sheep that was lost." Just so, I tell you, there will be more joy in heaven over one sinner who repents than over ninety-nine righteous persons who need no repentance. (Luke 15:4–7)

Love God and Love Others

A Pharisee asked Jesus which is the greatest commandment. Jesus said, "You shall love the Lord your God with all your heart, and with all your soul, and with all your mind. And a second is like it: You shall love your neighbor as yourself. On these two commandments depend all the Law and the Prophets" (Matthew 22:37–40).

No One Knows the Day and the Hour Jesus Will Return; There Will Be Rapture of His People

Jesus's apostles asked him what would be the signs of his return. Jesus said,

> But concerning that day and hour no one knows, not even the angels of heaven, nor the Son, but the Father only. For as were the days of Noah, so will be the coming of the Son of Man. For as in those days before the flood they were eating and drinking, marrying and giving in marriage, until the day when Noah entered the ark, and they were unaware until the flood came and swept them all away, so will be the coming of the Son of Man. Then two men will be on the field; one will be taken and one left. Two women will be grinding at the mill; one will be taken and one left. Therefore, stay awake, for you do not know on what day your Lord is coming. But know this, that if the master of the house had known in what part of the night the thief was coming, he would have stayed awake and would not let his house be broken into. Therefore you must also be ready, for the Son of Man is coming at an hour you do not expect. (Matthew 24:36–44)

We Will Be Judged Based on How We Treat Others

Jesus said,

> When the Son of Man comes in his glory, and all the angels with him, then he will sit on his glorious throne. Before him will be gathered all the nations, and he will separate people from one another as a shepherd separates the sheep from the goats. And he will place the sheep on the right, but the goats on the left. Then the King will say to those on his right, "Come, you who are blessed by my Father, inherit the kingdom prepared for you from the foundation of the world. For I was hungry and you gave me food, I was thirsty and you gave me drink, I was

a stranger and you welcomed me, I was naked and you clothed me, I was sick and you visited me, I was in prison and you came to me." Then the righteous will answer him saying, "Lord, when did we see you hungry and feed you, or thirsty and give you drink? And when did we see you a stranger and welcome you, or naked and clothe you?" And the King will answer them, "Truly, I say to you, as you did it to the least of these my brothers, you did it to me." (Matthew 25:31–46)

Then he will say to those on his left, "Depart from me, you cursed, into the eternal fire prepared for the devil and his angels. For I was hungry and you gave me no food, I was thirsty and you gave me no drink, I was a stranger and you did not welcome me, naked and you did not clothe me, sick and in prison and you did not visit me." Then they will also answer, saying "Lord, when did we see you hungry or thirsty, or a stranger, or naked or sick or in prison, and did not minister to you?" And then he will answer them, saying, "Truly, I say to you, as you did not do it to one of the least of these, you did not do it to me." And these will go away into eternal punishment, but the righteous into eternal life. (Matthew 25:41–46)

Christians Must Love and Be Kind to Everyone, Including Our Enemies

Jesus said,

But I say to you who hear, Love your enemies, do good to those who hate you, bless those who curse you, pray for those who abuse you. To the one who strikes you on the cheek, offer the other also, and from one who takes away your cloak do not withhold your tunic either. Give to everyone who begs from you and from the one who takes away your goods do not demand them back. And as you wish others would do to you, do so to them.

If you love those who love you, what benefit is that to you? For even sinners love those who love them. And if you do good to those who do good to you, what benefit is that to you? For even sinners do the same. And if you lend to those from whom you expect to receive, what credit is that to you? Even sinners lend to sinners, to get back the same amount. But love your enemies, and do good, and lend, expecting nothing in return, *and your reward will be great, and you will be sons of the Most High, for he is kind to the ungrateful and the evil. Be merciful, even as your Father is merciful.* (Luke 6:27–36)

The Most Important Passage in All of the Bible

Jesus said,

For God so loved the world, that he gave his only Son, that whoever believes in him should not perish but have eternal life. For God did not send his Son in to the world to condemn the world, but in order that the world might be saved through him. Whoever believes in him is not condemned, but whoever does not believe is condemned already, because he has not believed in the name of the only Son of God. And this is the judgment: the light has come into the world, and people loved the darkness rather than the light because their works were evil. For everyone who does wicked things hates the light and does not come to the light, lest his works should be exposed. But whoever does what is true comes to the light, so that it may be clearly seen that his works have been carried out in God. (John 3:16–21)

God the Father Will Save Anyone Who Loves and Follows His Son, Jesus

Jesus said to the crowds,

> I am the bread of life; whoever comes to me shall not hunger, and whoever believes in me shall never thirst. But I said to you that you have seen me and yet do not believe. All that the Father gives me will come to me, and *whoever comes to me I will never cast out.* For I have come down from heaven, not to do my own will but the will of him who sent me. And this is the will of him who sent me, that I should lose nothing of all that he has given me, but raise it up on the last day. *For this is the will of my Father, that everyone who looks on the Son and believes in him should have eternal life, and I will raise him up on the last day.* (John 6:35–40)

If You Follow God, No One Can Take You Away from Him

Jesus said,

> My sheep hear my voice, and I know them, and they follow me. I give them eternal life, and they will never perish, and no one will snatch them out of my hand. My Father, who has given them to me, is greater than all, and no one is able to snatch them out of the Father's hand. I and the Father are one. (John 10:27–30)

Jesus Is Our Resurrection and Life

Jesus said to Martha, the sister of Lazarus, before Jesus rose him from the dead, "I am the resurrection and the life. Whoever believes in me, though he die, yet shall he live, and everyone who lives and believes in me shall never die" (John 11:25–26).

God Considers Us Great When We Serve Others, Just as He Serves Us

Jesus said, "But whoever should be great among you must be your servant, and whoever would be first among you must be slave of all. For even the Son of Man came not to be served but to serve, and to give his life as a ransom for many" (Mark 10:43–45).

We Know We Are Followers of Jesus When We Love One Another

Jesus gave a new commandment to follow. "A new commandment I give you, that you love one another: just as I have loved you, you are also to love one another. By this all people will know that you are my followers, if you have love for one another" (John 13:34–35).

Jesus Will Take Those Who Follow Him to Heaven with Him

Jesus said,

> Let not your hearts be troubled. Believe in God; believe also in me. In my Father's house there are many rooms. If it were not so, would I have told you that I go to prepare a place for you? And if I go and prepare a place for you, I will come again and will take you to myself, that where I am you may be also. And you know the way to where I am going. (John 14:1–3)

If You Love Jesus and Follow What He Says to Do, the Holy Spirit Will Live in You and Help You

Jesus said,

> If you love me, you will keep my commandments. And I will ask the Father, and he will give you another Helper, to be with you forever, even the Spirit of Truth, whom the world cannot receive, because it neither sees him nor knows him. You know him, for he dwells with you and will be in you. (John 14:15–17)

Chapter 18

The Events That Led to Jesus Being Crucified

Jesus, who always existed as God, also became man and came to earth so he could take our sins off us, put them on him, and get punished to death in our place with our sins on him. This makes us sinless in God's eyes when we accept that Jesus did this wonderful thing to save us and then follow him in our daily lives. Therefore, Jesus came here to die. This was accomplished by Jesus being crucified. How did he get crucified?

At the time, the Jewish religious leaders were doing many things that God did not want them to do. They were adding their own man-made rules that God did not want on top of God's rules that he gave the people. They were also hypocrites. They demanded the people to follow these difficult rules, some of which they themselves did not follow. They did this to benefit themselves and not the people they were supposed to serve.

Jesus harshly and frequently criticized the religious leaders for doing this. Additionally, the religious leaders were jealous of Jesus. He did unprecedented miracles and taught with unparalleled wisdom and authority (because he was actually God). Some people were turning away from the Jewish religious leaders and following Jesus.

In their anger and jealousy, they decided to kill Jesus when they got the chance. These are some of the events that the religious leaders used as an excuse to kill Jesus. They are not necessarily in order as presented in the Bible.

One day, a paralytic man was brought to Jesus to be healed. Jesus said to the man, "Take heart my son, your sins are forgiven" (Mark 2:5). Some of the religious leaders heard this and said, "He is blaspheming! Who can forgive sins but God alone?" (Mark 2:7). (Jesus is God, but the religious leaders did not believe it.)

Jesus came to save us because we are all sinners. Therefore, Jesus spent a lot of time with people who were known to be big sinners because he was teaching them. He said, "A well person does not need a doctor, but a sick person does."

Jesus was the doctor, helping those who came to him who were sick with sin. The religious leaders of the time were full of pride, and they thought they were better and holier than everyone else was. They did not speak with people known to be sinners (but should have). They were upset and disgusted with Jesus for associating with sinners. Sinners were the people Jesus came to save ... which is *all of us.*

One day, Jesus cast a demon out of a man who was possessed. The Pharisees (religious leaders) were upset and jealous because they did not have the power to cast demons out of people. They began to tell others that Jesus was able to cast demons out of people because he was a demon himself (a lie).

Jesus entered a church, and there was a man there with a crippled hand. Jesus was about to heal the man. It was the Sabbath (either a Saturday or a Sunday). The Pharisees asked Jesus, "Is it lawful to heal a person on the Sabbath?"

They did this because they wanted to accuse Jesus of breaking the commandment "You shall keep the Sabbath holy," which meant that, not only should you go to church on the Sabbath, you should not do work on that day.

Jesus said to them, "Which one of you who has a sheep, if it falls into a pit on the Sabbath, would not take hold of it and lift it out? Of how much more value is a man than a sheep! So it is lawful to do good on the Sabbath" (Matthew 12:11–12).

Jesus then healed the man with the crippled hand. The Pharisees got together and used this event in planning on how to destroy Jesus.

Jesus said to the people, "Beware of the scribes [some of the religious leaders at the time] who like to walk around in long robes and like greetings in marketplaces and have the best seats in the churches and the places of honor at feasts, who devour widows' savings, and for money they make long prayers. They will receive the greater punishment." This, of course, made the priests mad at Jesus (Matthew 23).

Jesus Harshly Condemns the Religious Leaders

> While Jesus was speaking, a Pharisee asked him to dine with him, so he went in and reclined at table. The Pharisee was astonished to see that he did not first wash before dinner. And the Lord said to him "Now you Pharisees cleanse the outside of the cup and of the dish, but inside you are full of greed and wickedness. You fools! Did not he who made the outside make the inside also? But give as alms those things that are within, and behold, everything is clean for you.
>
> "But woe to you Pharisees! For you tithe mint and rue and every herb, and neglect justice and the love of God. These you ought to have done, without neglecting the others. Woe to you Pharisees! For you love the best seat in the synagogues and greetings in the marketplaces. Woe to you! For you are like unmarked graves, and people walk over them without knowing it."
>
> One of the lawyers answered him, "Teacher, in saying these things you insult us also." And he said "Woe to you

lawyers also! For you load people with burdens hard to bear, and you yourselves do not touch the burdens with one of your fingers. Woe to you! For you build the tombs of the prophets your fathers killed. So you are witnesses and you consent to the deeds of your fathers, for they killed them, and you build their tombs. Therefore also the wisdom of God said 'I will send them prophets and apostles, some of whom they will kill and persecute, so that the blood of all the prophets, shed from the foundation of the world, may be charged against this generation, from the blood of Abel to the blood of Zechariah, who perished between the altar and the sanctuary.' Yes, I tell you, it will be required of this generation. Woe to you lawyers! For you have taken away the key of knowledge. You did not enter yourselves, and you hindered those who were entering."

As he went away from there, the scribes and the Pharisees began to press him hard and to provoke him to speak about many things, lying in wait for him, to catch him in something he might say. (Luke 11:37–54)

One of the things the religious leaders used against Jesus as an excuse to kill him was Jesus was healing people and doing good works on the Sabbath. One of the Ten Commandments is to keep the Sabbath holy. In the commandment, it says, "Six days you shall labor, do all your work, but on the seventh day you shall do no work" (Exodus 20:8–9).

One day on the Sabbath, Jesus came across a man who had been an invalid for thirty-eight years. Jesus felt compassion for the man, so he healed him, and now the man could walk. The religious leaders began persecuting Jesus for healing people on the Sabbath. Jesus told them that God made the Sabbath for man so man can have a day to rest from his regular work. It was *never* meant to stop people from doing good for others on that day. People should do good things for others, if necessary, *on any day*.

The religious leaders ignored this and held on to their statement that Jesus was breaking the law because he was doing work on the Sabbath by healing people. Jesus responded, "My Father is working until now, and I am working. This is why the Jews were seeking all the more to kill Jesus, because not only was he breaking the Sabbath, but he was even calling God his own Father, making himself equal with God" (John 5:17–18). (In truth, he was.)

Jesus Tells the Religious Leaders They Are from Their Father, the Devil; Jesus Then Publicly Declares That He Is God

Jesus and the religious leaders were increasingly at odds with each other. The leaders were envious of Jesus. They hated him also because Jesus clearly, truthfully, and *publicly* criticized the religious leaders for not following God's will. Instead they added human traditions to God's will that they used for their own benefit, at the expense of the people they were supposed to serve.

One day, the religious leaders and Jesus were in a public argument. The following is the explosive statements Jesus made against them.

Jesus said to them, "I know you are offspring of Abraham, yet you seek to kill me because my words find no place in you. I speak of what I have seen with my Father, and you do what you have heard from your father."

They answered him, "Abraham is our father."

Jesus said to them, "If you were Abraham's children, you would be doing the works Abraham did, but now you seek to kill me, a man who has told you the truth that I heard from God. This is not what Abraham did. You are doing the works your father did."

They said to him, "We are not born of sexual immorality. We have one Father—even God."

Jesus said to them,

If God were your Father, you would love me, for I came
from God and I am here. I came not of my own accord,
but he sent me. Why do you not understand what I say?
It is because you cannot bear to hear my word. You are of
your father the devil, and your will is to do your father's
desires. He was a murderer from the beginning, and has
nothing to do with the truth, because there is no truth in
him. When he lies, he speaks out of his own character,
for he is a liar, and the father of lies. But because I tell the
truth, you do not believe me. Which one of you convicts
me of sin? If I tell the truth, why do you not believe me?
Whoever is of God hears the words of God. The reason
why you do not hear them is that you are not of God.
(John 8:37–47)

The Jews responded by saying that Jesus was possessed by a demon, which
was why he was saying these things. Jesus replied that he did not have a
demon and anyone who kept his word would never see death.

The Jews then said that Jesus must have a demon in him. All of the
prophets eventually died, including Abraham. They asked him who he
thought he was. Did he think he was greater than Abraham? Jesus said
that God was his Father and that Abraham rejoiced that he would see the
day of Jesus come.

The Jewish religious leaders said, "You are not yet fifty years old. How did
you see Abraham?" (John 8:57).

Jesus's next statement was the one the Pharisees would use against him as
their main reason to crucify him. "Truly, truly, I say to you, *before Abraham
was, I am*" (John 8:58).

By Jesus saying "Before Abraham was, I AM," he was saying that he was
God. When God appeared to Moses and told him he would use him to
set the Jewish people free, Moses asked God, "What shall I tell the people
your name is?"

God responded, "I AM WHO I AM. Say this to the people of Israel, 'I AM has sent me to you'" (Exodus 3:14).

Therefore, Jesus was calling himself the same name that God told Moses to call him. At hearing this, the Jewish religious leaders picked up stones to throw at Jesus, but Jesus escaped and left.

Later, other Jews were gathered around Jesus. They said to him, "Don't keep us in suspense. Are you the Christ?"

Jesus responded, "I told you, and you do not believe. The works that I do in my Father's name bear witness about me, but you do not believe because you are not part of my flock. My sheep hear my voice, and I know them, and they follow me. I give them eternal life, and they will never perish, and no one will snatch them out of my hand. My Father, who has given them to me, is greater than all, and no one is able to snatch them out of the Father's hand. I and the father are one."

The Jews picked up stones again to stone him.

Jesus answered them, "I have shown you many good works from the Father; for which of them are you going to stone me?"

The Jews answered him, "It is not for a good work that we are going to stone you, *but for blasphemy, because you, being a man, make yourself God*" (John 10:24–33).

So Jesus was later put to death for telling the truth. They crucified him because Jesus said he was God. He is.

Caiaphas Decides Jesus Must Die

Many people were coming to believe in Jesus, which worried the Pharisees. The chief priests and Pharisees gathered together to discuss what to do.

They said, "What are we to do? For this man performs many signs. If we let him go on like this, everyone will believe in him, and the Romans will come and take away both our place and our nation" (John 11:47–48).

Caiaphas was the high priest that year. His statement in response to this is one of the most prophetic statements in the entire Bible. Caiaphas said, "You know nothing at all. Nor do you understand that *it is better for you that one man should die for the people, not that the whole nation should perish*" (John 11:49–50).

Caiaphas did not realize it, but he was prophesizing that it would be better if one man died for the sins of the world rather than the whole world die because of their sins.

Chapter 19

The Death and Resurrection of Jesus

The chief priests and elders of the people gathered in the palace of the high priest, Caiaphas. They plotted together to arrest Jesus secretly and kill him. However, to avoid an uproar among the people, they did not want to do it during the Passover feast.

Jesus and his apostles and disciples entered Jerusalem for the Passover feast. Jesus knew this Passover feast would end with his crucifixion in a few days. Jesus had two disciples get him a donkey to ride on into Jerusalem.

This was done to fulfill the Old Testament prophesy, "Rejoice greatly, O daughter of Zion! Shout aloud, O daughter of Jerusalem! Behold, your king is coming to you; righteousness and having salvation is he, humble and mounted on a donkey, on a colt, the foal of a donkey" (Zechariah 9:9).

Most of the crowd spread their cloaks on the road and put palm branches down for Jesus to walk on so his feet would not touch the ground. People were walking before him and after him shouting, "Hosanna to the Son of David! Blessed is he who comes in the name of the Lord! Hosanna in the highest!" (Matthew 21:9). The whole city was stirred up in joy and excitement at the entry of Jesus into Jerusalem. How things will change over the next few days.

Jesus told his apostles and disciples that he would soon be killed. For example, he told them that, when they entered Jerusalem, he would soon be delivered over to the chief priests and scribes. They would condemn him to death and deliver him to the Gentiles (Roman soldiers). He would be mocked and flogged (brutally whipped) and then crucified. After this, he would be raised on the third day. For whatever reason, the apostles were unable to either understand or believe these things Jesus was telling them about his upcoming suffering and death.

Jesus gave directions to his disciples on where they would prepare a room for the Passover. This would come to be known as the Last Supper. The apostles were directed to a large upper room for this. As they were eating, Jesus then told his twelve apostles that one of them would betray him.

The apostles were all surprised, and they did not know which one of them it could be. John asked Jesus who would betray him, and he revealed to him it would be Judas. Judas previously went to the chief priests in order to betray Jesus to them. They promised to give him money for this, and Judas looked for an opportunity to betray Jesus.

> And as they were eating, he took bread, and after blessing it broke it and gave it to them, and said "This is my body." And he took a cup, and when he had given thanks he gave it to them, "This is the blood of the covenant, which is poured out for many. Truly, I say to you, I will not drink again of the fruit of the vine until that day when I drink it new in the kingdom of God." (Mark 14:22–25)

After the Last Supper, they all went out to the Mount of Olives.

Jesus said to them, "You will all fall away, for it is written, 'I will strike the shepherd, and the sheep will be scattered.' But after I am raised up, I will go before you to Galilee."

Peter said to him, "Even though they all fall away, I will not."

And Jesus said to him, "Truly, I tell you, this very night, before the rooster crows twice, you will deny me three times." But he said emphatically, "If I must die with you, I will not deny you." And they all said the same (Mark 14:26–31).

Jesus went with his disciples to a place called Gethsemane to pray. He took Peter, James, and John alone with him. He told them, "My soul is very sorrowful, even to death; remain here and watch with me" (Matthew 26:38).

Jesus walked away a little bit, fell on his face, and prayed, "My father, if it is possible, let this cup pass from me; nevertheless, not as I will, but as you will" (Matthew 26:39).

Jesus returned and found the apostles asleep. He woke them up, told them to be on guard, and returned to praying. He said, "My Father, if this cannot pass unless I drink it, your will be done" (Matthew 26:42).

Jesus returned to the apostles and found them sleeping again. He went and prayed to the Father a third time, saying the same thing. He then returned to the apostles and told them to wake up because his betrayer was at hand.

Judas knew where Jesus would be at. He came to the garden of Gethsemane with a band of soldiers and some officers from the chief priests and Pharisees. Judas drew near to kiss Jesus, which was his signal to the soldiers of identifying which one was Jesus.

Jesus said to him, "Judas, would you betray the Son of Man with a kiss?" (Luke 22:48). Jesus then walked forward and said to them, "Who do you seek?"

They said, "Jesus of Nazareth."

Jesus said to them, "I am he." (John 18:4–5).

When he said this, the whole crowd drew back and fell to the ground from the power that came out of Jesus when he spoke.

Jesus asked them again, "Whom do you seek?"

They said, "Jesus of Nazareth."

Jesus said, "I told you I am he, so if you seek me, let these others go" (John 18:7–8).

They listened to Jesus, apparently fearful of the power that just came out of him, and knocked them over. This fulfilled a prophesy that Jesus earlier gave. "Of those whom you gave me I have not lost one" (John 18:9).

At this, to defend Jesus, Peter pulled out his sword, struck the high priest's servant, and cut off his ear.

Jesus told Peter to put his sword away, saying, "Shall I not drink the cup that the Father has given me?" (John 18:11).

The band of soldiers and officers arrested Jesus and took him to the Jewish religious leaders that ordered Jesus's arrest. The head of this was Caiaphas, the high priest.

The chief priests and the whole council were looking for any kind of testimony they could use against Jesus to put him to death. Many false witnesses came forward, but their testimonies contradicted each other. Jesus remained silent during all of the testimony against him. Remember, he came here to die in our place, not to defend himself from a death sentence.

The high priest then said to him, "I adjure you by the living God, tell us if you are the Christ, the Son of God."

Jesus said to him, "You have said so, But I tell you, from now on you will see the Son of man seated at the right hand of Power and coming on the clouds of heaven" (Matthew 26:63–64).

The high priest tore his robes and said that Jesus uttered blasphemy and they needed no more witnesses since everyone heard his blasphemy. He asked the religious leaders, "What is your judgment?"

They answered, "He deserves death." Then they spit in his face and struck him. And some slapped him, saying, "Prophesy to us, you Christ! Who is it that struck you?" (Matthew 26:65–68).

Earlier in the day, before Jesus was arrested, the apostles were arguing amongst themselves as to which one of them would be considered the greatest apostle. Jesus entered their prideful and arrogant conversation, and he confronted Peter. He told Peter that, before this day was over, before the rooster crowed, he would deny knowing Jesus three times.

Peter said this would absolutely not happen. He said he would follow Jesus anywhere he would go, even to death. Jesus reaffirmed that Peter would in fact deny knowing him three times before the rooster crowed today.

Now, Jesus was being tried by the religious leaders inside an official building, while Peter hung outside by the crowd, warming himself by a fire.

A servant girl approached Peter and said, "This man was with Jesus."

Peter said he did not know what she was talking about, and he moved to another spot.

Then another servant girl recognized Peter and said, "This man was with Jesus."

Peter took an oath, swearing that he did not know Jesus.

Shortly after, some bystanders came up to him and said, "We can tell by your accent that you are one of the followers with Jesus."

Peter got angry and started swearing and cursing, saying, "I don't know the man!"

And immediately, while he was still speaking, the rooster crowed. And Jesus looked at Peter. And Peter remembered the saying of the Lord, how he said to him, "Before the rooster crows today, you will deny me three times." And Peter went out and wept bitterly (Mark 14:66–72; Luke 22:60–62).

The men who were holding Jesus in custody were making fun of him as they spit on him and beat him. They blindfolded Jesus and kept asking him as they hit him, "Prophesy to us, you Christ! Who is it that struck you?" (Matthew 26:68). And they said many other things against him as they hit him, blaspheming him.

Jesus was now brought before Pontius Pilate, the Roman governor who was in charge of Jerusalem. The religious leaders who brought Jesus to Pilate told the governor that they brought Jesus to him because he was misleading the nation of Israel, forbidding the people to pay taxes to Caesar (lies), and saying that he was the Christ and a king (the truth).

Pilate questioned Jesus. After thoroughly questioning him, Pilate then told the chief priests and the crowds that he did not find Jesus guilty of anything.

The religious leaders kept telling Pilate that Jesus was a troublemaker and he was stirring up the crowds. Pilate found out that Jesus was from Galilee. King Herod was the ruler of Galilee. Pilate did not want to have anything to do with judging Jesus. He knew that Jesus was an innocent man and the Jewish religious leaders were doing all of this because they were envious of Jesus.

He told the Jewish religious leaders that, since Jesus was a Galilean, he fell under King Herod's jurisdiction, and Herod was the one that needed to hear their case against Jesus. The Jewish religious leaders brought Jesus to King Herod, hoping that Herod would find him guilty and sentence him to die.

King Herod was excited to see Jesus. He heard a lot about him, and he wanted to see Jesus perform miracles for him. Herod questioned Jesus, but

Jesus remained silent. The chief priests and scribes kept making accusations against Jesus to Herod.

No matter what was said to Jesus or about him, he remained silent. Remember, he came here to die with our sins on him to save us. He did not want to get out of a death sentence. So he remained quiet and never defended himself during this whole ordeal.

King Herod became upset that Jesus would not perform a miracle for him and he would not speak. He dressed Jesus in fancy clothes to make fun of him, and then he sent him back to Pilate.

When Jesus was brought back to Pilate, he brought Jesus in to talk with him again. He asked Jesus, "Are you the King of the Jews? Your own nation and the chief priests have delivered you over to me. What have you done?"

Jesus answered, "My kingdom is not of this world. If my kingdom were of this world, my servants would have been fighting, that I might not be delivered over to the Jews. But my kingdom is not from the world."

Then Pilate said to him, "So you are a king?"

Jesus answered, "You say that I am a king. For this purpose I was born and for this purpose I have come into the world—to bear witness to the truth. Everyone who is of the truth listens to my voice" (John 18:33–37).

Pilate made an announcement to the chief priests and the people,

> You brought Jesus to me, accusing him of misleading the people. I have thoroughly examined him. *I did not find this man guilty of any of the charges you made against him. Neither did King Herod. Nothing deserving death has been done by Jesus.* Therefore, I will punish him, and set him free. (Luke 23:13–17)

The religious leaders would not stop demanding that Pilate condemn Jesus. Pilate tried to set Jesus free. He knew that Jesus was innocent of the charges that the religious leaders accused him of, and they only wanted Jesus killed out of their envy of him. Pilate gave the crowd a choice of one prisoner that he would set free as a Passover tradition, Jesus or a murderer and insurrectionist named Barabbas. Pilate thought that the people would want Jesus set free instead of Barabbas. The religious leaders convinced the crowd to tell Pilate they wanted Barabbas released instead of Jesus, which Pilate did.

Pilate made another attempt to save Jesus's life from the envious religious leaders and the bloodthirsty crowd they stirred up. He had Jesus severely flogged, or whipped. This split Jesus's back open. After Jesus was flogged, the soldiers brought him inside the governor's headquarters. They put a purple cloak on him to make fun of him that he was a king. They made a crown of thorns and put it on his head.

They hit him in the head with a reed, spit on him, and made fun of him by bowing down and saying, "Hail, King of the Jews!" (Matthew 27:29). When they were done whipping him and beating him, scripture says he was beaten so badly that he was not recognizable as a human being.

Pilate brought Jesus back out to the crowd. Jesus was beaten so badly that Pilate hoped the crowd would feel he was punished enough and they would not want him killed.

Pilate showed Jesus to the crowd and shouted, "Behold the man!" (John 19:5), which meant "Look at him! Isn't he punished *enough?*"

The chief priests screamed out, "Crucify him!"

Pilate decided to release Jesus anyway because he found no guilt in him. Then the religious leaders backed Pilate into a corner.

They said, "Jesus says he is a king. We have no king but Caesar. If you release this man, you are no friend of Caesar" (John 19:12).

Caesar was the supreme leader of Rome and its conquered territories (Israel). If it got out that Pontius Pilate released a man who claimed to be the king of Israel in place of Caesar, Caesar might have Pilate executed.

"So when Pilate saw that he was gaining nothing, but rather that a riot was beginning, he took water and washed his hands before the crowd, saying, 'I am innocent of this man's blood; see to it yourselves.' Then he delivered Jesus up to be crucified" (Matthew 27:24–26).

Jesus was led away by the Roman soldiers and made to carry his cross. They forced a man named Simon of Cyrene to help Jesus carry his cross. They brought Jesus, along with two other criminals who were to be crucified, to a place called Golgotha, which means "place of a skull."

A great multitude of people and groups of women were following Jesus, grieving for him for what was happening to him. It was there that they crucified Jesus, along with one of the criminals on his right and one on his left.

As they were crucifying Jesus, he said, "Father forgive them, for they know not what they do" (Luke 23:34).

Pontius Pilate wrote an inscription and put it on the cross of Jesus. It said, "Jesus of Nazareth, the King of the Jews" (John 19:19). It was written in Aramaic, Latin, and Greek so everyone could read it.

They offered him wine mixed with gall to drink, but when he tasted it, he would not drink it. The Roman soldiers divided Jesus's garments among them. But his tunic was seamless, woven in one piece from top to bottom. They could not tear it to divide it, so they cast lots for it, to see who would get it.

The rulers mocked Jesus, saying, "He saved others; let him save himself, if he is the Christ of God, his Chosen one!" (Luke 23:35).

"Aha! You who would destroy the temple and rebuild it in three days, save yourself, and come down from the cross!" (Mark 15:29–30).

The Roman soldiers and the two criminals crucified on both sides of Jesus said the same thing at first. One of the criminals then said, "If you are the Christ, save yourself and save us too!"

The other criminal came to believe in Jesus. He said, "Don't you fear God? We deserve our punishment for our bad deeds, but Jesus has done nothing wrong."

The criminal then said, "Jesus, remember me when you come into your kingdom."

And Jesus said to the criminal, "Truly, I say to you, today you will be with me in Paradise" (Luke 23:42–43).

Standing by the cross of Jesus were his mother; his mother's sister, Mary, the wife of Clopas; and Mary Magdalene. When Jesus saw his mother and the disciple whom he loved (the apostle John) standing nearby, he said to his mother, "Woman, behold your son!" Then he said to the disciple, "Behold, your mother!"

And from that day on, the apostle John took her into his own home (John 19:25–27).

Between the sixth and ninth hour, the sun's light failed, and there was darkness over the whole land. In the ninth hour, Jesus cried out with a loud voice, saying, "My God, My God, why have you forsaken me?" (Matthew 27:45–46).

One of the bystanders filled a sponge with sour wine and gave it to Jesus to drink, saying, "Let's see if Elijah will come and take him down" (Mark 15:36).

After Jesus drank the sour wine, he said, "It is finished" (John 19:30). "Then Jesus, calling out with a loud voice, said, 'Father, into your hands I commit my spirit!' And having said this he breathed his last" (Luke 23:46–47).

> Since it was the day of Preparation, and so that the bodies would not remain on the cross on the Sabbath (for that Sabbath was a high day), the Jews asked Pilate that their legs might be broken and they might be taken away. So the soldiers came and broke the legs of the first, and of the other who had been crucified with him. But when they came to Jesus and saw that he was already dead, they did not break his legs. But one of the soldiers pierced his side with a spear, and at once there came out blood and water. For these things took place that the Scripture might be fulfilled: "Not one of his bones will be broken." And again another Scripture says, "They will look on him who they pierced." (John 19:31–37)

As this happened, the curtain in the temple was split in two from top to bottom. There were earthquakes, and rocks split open. People who had died got out of their graves. After Jesus's resurrection, these people who got out of their graves walked around the city and appeared to many people.

When the centurion and those who were with Jesus during all of this saw the earthquakes and everything that took place, they were filled with awe and said, "Truly this was the Son of God!" (Matthew 27:54).

Many in the crowds who saw all of these events went home sad and mourning for what happened to Jesus. Many women who followed Jesus from Galilee were there, along with other women who came up from Jerusalem, who had been ministering to him. These included Mary Magdalene, Mary, the mother of James and Joseph, and the mother of the sons of Zebedee.

There was a rich man named Joseph from Arimathea who was a member of the council. He did not vote that Jesus was guilty, and he came to believe in Jesus. Joseph asked Pontius Pilate if he could have Jesus's body to bury it, and Pilate granted it to him. Joseph buried Jesus in his own tomb, which was a new tomb cut out of rock.

The next day, the Pharisees went to Pontius Pilate. They told him that Jesus kept saying that he would rise three days after he died. They thought Jesus's disciples might steal Jesus's body to make it look like he rose from the dead. They asked Pilate if he could secure Jesus's tomb. Pilate gave them a guard of soldiers and told the Pharisees to make Jesus's tomb as secure as they could. They sealed a stone over the tomb and placed Roman soldiers around it to guard it.

The Resurrection of Jesus

On the first day of the week, a group of women who knew Jesus went to his tomb with spices they prepared. When they got there, an earthquake took place because an angel of the Lord descended from heaven and rolled away the stone covering the tomb. He was sitting on it. His appearance was like lightning, and his clothes were as white as snow. When this happened, "For fear of him the guards trembled and became like dead men" (Matthew 28:4).

Jesus's body was gone from the tomb, and it was empty. The angel said to the women,

> Do not be afraid, for I know that you seek Jesus who was crucified. He is not here, for he has risen, as he said. Come, see the place where he lay. Then go quickly and tell his disciples that he has risen from the dead, and behold, he is going before you to Galilee; there you will see him. See, I have told you. (Matthew 28:5–7)

The woman ran with great joy to tell the apostles. Jesus appeared to the women and said, "Greetings! Do not be afraid; go and tell my brothers to go to Galilee, and there they will see me" (Matthew 28:9–10). The women grabbed Jesus and worshipped him. Then they went to tell the disciples.

The soldiers guarding the tomb came to the religious leaders and told them what happened. The religious leaders gave them a bunch of money and told them to tell the people that the apostles snuck in and stole his body while they were all asleep. This was done to try to prevent the people from believing the news that Jesus rose from the dead, but it didn't work well.

The apostles were gathered together, hiding out in fear of the Jews that crucified Jesus. Jesus appeared in their midst. He said, "'Peace be with You. As the Father has sent me, even so I am sending you.' And when he had said this, he breathed on them and said to them, 'Receive the Holy Spirit. If you forgive the sins of any, they are forgiven of them; if you withhold forgiveness from any, it is withheld'" (John 20:21–22).

Thomas was not with them when Jesus appeared. He would not believe them that Jesus appeared to them. He said, unless he was able to see the nail marks in his hands and place his hand in Jesus's side where he was stabbed with a spear on the cross, he wouldn't believe it was Jesus.

Eight days later, the apostles were together again, and Thomas was with them this time. Jesus appeared to all of them and said, "Peace be with you" (John 20:26).

He told Thomas to put his finger into the nail holes in his hands and his hand into his side. "Thomas answered him, 'My Lord and My God!' Jesus said to him, 'Have you believed because you have seen me? Blessed are those who have not seen and yet believed'" (John 20:28–29).

Jesus appeared to the apostles once again. He sat down and had a talk with Peter. When Jesus was arrested and on trial leading to his crucifixion, Peter denied knowing Jesus three times out of fear of also being arrested.

In this conversation with Peter after Jesus was resurrected, he allowed Peter to make up for the three times that he denied knowing him.

Jesus asked Peter three times, "Peter, do you love me?"

Peter responded three times, "Yes, Lord, I love you."

This allowed him to make up for denying Jesus three times. After each time Peter said that he loved him, Jesus responded, "If you love me, feed my sheep" (John 21:15–19).

We are Jesus's sheep. He is our Good Shepherd. Jesus was telling Peter that if you love Jesus, you need to love and take care of other people. That is our job as followers of Jesus, to love and to care for other people.

At another time when Jesus appeared to the apostles after he rose from the dead, he gave them the Great Commission, the instructions he wants his followers (us) to do. Jesus said,

> All authority in heaven and on earth has been given to me. Go therefore and make disciples of all nations, baptizing them in the name of the Father and of the Son and of the Holy Spirit, teaching them to observe all that I have commanded you. And behold, I am with you always, to the end of the age. (Matthew 28:18–20)

"Go into all the world and proclaim the gospel to the whole creation. Whoever believes and is baptized will be saved, but whoever does not believe will be condemned" (Mark 16:15–16).

After Jesus rose from the dead, he appeared to the apostles and other people multiple times over a forty-day period. On one occasion, he appeared to a crowd of over five hundred people.

Jesus then told the apostles that he would now return to heaven. When he left, the Holy Spirit (God) would then come down and live inside each of them, giving them power, strength, and guidance.

After Jesus said these things, as the apostles were looking at him, Jesus was lifted up, and a cloud took him out of their sight. As the apostles were watching Jesus being lifted up into heaven, two angels wearing white robes appeared to them. They said, "Men of Galilee, why do you stand looking into heaven? This Jesus, who was taken up from you into heaven, will come in the same way as you saw him go into heaven" (Acts 1:11).

Chapter 20

The Apostles and the Rise of the Christian Church

Shortly after Jesus returned to heaven, the apostles were gathered together in a group. Suddenly a sound came from heaven that sounded like a mighty wind, and a flame of fire hovered above each of the apostle's heads. It was the Holy Spirit, which came to live inside each of the apostles.

The Holy Spirit is the third person of God (the Father, the Son [Jesus], and the Holy Spirit). The Holy Spirit gave the apostles strength, wisdom, power, and encouragement to go out and tell everybody who Jesus is and how everyone can be saved and go to heaven when he or she dies. The good news is that, when we accept Jesus as our Savior and follow him, the Holy Spirit comes and lives in us and guides us on our lives.

The apostles traveled around Israel, telling everyone about Jesus and how to be saved by him. They performed many miracles such as healing the sick and making the paralyzed walk and the blind see. Thousands of people believed in their message about Jesus, and they accepted Jesus as their God and were saved.

The religious leaders who killed Jesus because they were jealous of him were angry at the apostles for telling the Israelites to follow Jesus as their God. They kept arresting the apostles and ordering them to stop talking about Jesus. The Holy Spirit was living inside of the apostles. He guided the apostles on what they said to the religious leaders. The apostles amazed the religious leaders in their wise and courageous responses to them, which caused these leaders to keep letting the apostles go after they arrested them.

Jesus Comes to Paul

There was a Jewish religious leader named Saul. He was relentless in his efforts to try to get rid of the followers of Jesus. He entered house after house, dragging off men and women and sending them to prison if they followed Jesus.

One day, Saul was on his way to Damascus, Syria, to arrest any followers of Jesus he could find. As he approached Damascus, a light from heaven flashed around him, and it knocked him to the ground. He then heard a voice saying, "Saul, Saul, why are you persecuting me?"

Saul said, "Who are you, Lord?"

The voice said, "I am Jesus, who you are persecuting. But rise and enter the city, and you will be told what you are to do" (Acts 9:3–6).

Saul got up, but he was unable to see. He was led around by the hand by the men he was with because he was now blind.

God came to a disciple of Jesus named Ananias. He told Ananias where to go to find a man named Saul. He was to lay his hands on Saul so he would regain his sight.

Ananias said to God, "A lot of people told me about this man named Saul, how much evil he has done to the people that follow Jesus."

God said, "Go to meet him because he is a chosen instrument of mine. He will tell the Gentiles and the kings and the children of Israel all about me."

Ananias went to Saul, laid hands on him, and said, "Brother Saul, the Lord Jesus who appeared to you on the road by which you came has sent me so that you may regain your sight and be filled by the Holy Spirit."

Immediately, Saul could see again. He was filled with the Holy Spirit, which energized him to go out and tell everyone about Jesus (Acts 9:10–19).

From this point on, Saul's name was changed to Paul. Paul started to teach in all the churches that Jesus was the Son of God and he came here to save everyone from his or her sins. The religious leaders who killed Jesus got mad about this and tried to kill Paul.

But God was with Paul, and he always helped him escape. Paul did many miracles so people would believe that Jesus was with him. For example, he healed people who were very sick, and he brought back to life a woman who recently died.

Around the same time, Peter was also teaching everyone about Jesus. He saw the Holy Spirit come down and fall on the Gentiles (people who are not Jews)(us). He was told that God wanted to save the whole world from their sins so they could get to heaven when they die, not just the Jews.

The religious leaders who killed Jesus were becoming increasingly angry at the apostles and disciples who were teaching people about Jesus. They killed the apostle James. They captured Peter and put him in prison. He was put in chains in the prison, and four squads of soldiers were guarding him.

But Peter's friends were praying to God that God would save Peter. One night, Peter was sleeping between two soldiers. He was tied up with two chains, and guards were guarding him at his prison door.

All of a sudden, an angel of the Lord appeared. He stood next to Peter, and a heavenly light shone in the prison cell.

The angel woke up Peter and said, "Get up quickly."

The chains immediately fell off Peter's hands. The angel told Peter to follow him, and he did. God then opened up the doors of the prison, and Peter and the angel walked past all of the guards, who God put to sleep.

They walked out into the street, and the angel left Peter (Acts 12:6–11). Peter then returned to teaching the people of Israel about Jesus.

Peter was the main person who started the Christian churches in Israel and the surrounding areas. Around the same time, the apostle Paul was also teaching the crowds about Jesus. Paul, more than anyone else, spread the message about Jesus all over the world. His teachings eventually led the Roman Empire to follow Jesus, a main way that Christianity spread throughout the world.

The Jewish religious leaders were against the teachings of Jesus since they were the ones that killed him. They tried to stop Paul from teaching about Jesus. They captured Paul and stoned him. (They threw stones at him until they believed that he was dead.)

Thinking that they killed Paul, the religious leaders left after they stoned him. The Spirit of God came to Paul and healed him from the stoning. Paul stood up and went right back into the city, and he taught more people about Jesus.

Because of this, the religious leaders (the Pharisees and Saducees) captured Paul again along with his friend Silas. They beat them with sticks and chained them up in prison. Paul and Silas were praying and singing songs about God in prison.

God then caused a big earthquake to happen. All of the doors of the prison opened up, and the chains fell off Paul and Silas.

When the prison guard saw what God did, he asked Paul and Silas, "Sirs, what must I do to be saved?"

They said, "Believe in the Lord Jesus, and you will be saved, you and your family."

The prison guard brought Paul and Silas to his home. The guard's whole family was told about Jesus, and they decided to follow and trust in him.

They were baptized by Paul and Silas, and they were saved from their sins (Acts 16:25–34).

After this, Paul traveled to many cities and countries, teaching that following Jesus is the way to save themselves from sin and to get to heaven one day. Some people did not believe what Paul taught about Jesus. Many did, however, and were saved.

Due to teaching about Jesus, the religious leaders captured Paul and put him in prison for two years. Although it might have seemed like a tragedy, it was actually a huge benefit for Paul and all of us that he was put in prison for a long time.

He was able to write several extremely important letters while he was in prison because he had a lot of free time with not much else to do. These letters became a major part of the New Testament in the Bible. They taught us so much about God, his plans for us, and the things he wants us to do. We will now read sections of the important letters of Paul written to the various churches of the time.

Chapter 21

Letters of the Apostles to the New Christians

The Letter of Paul to the Romans

"There will be trouble and distress for every human being who does evil, but glory and honor and peace for everyone who does good" (Romans 2:9–11).

"God's gift to us is that if we put our faith into Jesus to save us from our sins, God will forgive all of our sins and see us as righteous" (Romans 3:21–26).

"We rejoice in our sufferings, knowing that suffering produces endurance, and endurance produces character, and character produces hope, and hope does not put us to shame, because God's love has been poured into our hearts through the Holy Spirit who has been given to us" (Romans 5:3).

Sin and death entered the whole world by the sinning of just one man, Adam. Likewise, one man saved the whole world from sin by the gift of his accepting punishment for our sins, Jesus Christ.

"Therefore, as one trespass led to condemnation for all men, so one act of righteousness leads to justification and life for all men. For as by the one man's disobedience the many were made sinners, so by the one man's obedience the many will be made righteous. Now the law came in to increase the trespass, but where sin increased, grace abounded all the more, so that, as sin reigned in death, grace also might reign through righteousness leading to eternal life through Jesus Christ our Lord" (Romans 5:18–21).

"We received the spirit of adoption as children of God, who is our father. The Holy Spirit Himself bears witness to our spirit that we are children of God, and if children, then heirs- heirs of God and fellow heirs with Jesus Christ" (Romans 8:15–17).

Our spirits groan inside us because they cannot wait to be with God in heaven. In heaven, we will be adopted children of God, living in redeemed heavenly bodies (Romans 8:18–25). If we don't know exactly what to pray for, ask God to guide us on what to pray for, and the Holy Spirit will help us (Romans 8:26–27).

"And we know that for those who love God all things work together for good, for those who are called according to his purpose. For those whom he foreknew he also predestined to be conformed to the image of his Son, in order that he may be the firstborn among many brothers. And those who he predestined he also called, and those whom he called he also justified, and those whom he justified he also glorified" (Romans 8:28–30).

"If God is for us, who can be against us? He who did not spare his own Son but gave him up for us all, how will he not also with him graciously give us all things?" (Romans 8:31–32).

Nothing can separate us from God and his love for us (Romans 8:35–39).

"If you confess with your mouth that Jesus is Lord and believe in your heart that God raised him from the dead, you will be saved. For the scripture says 'Everyone who believes in Jesus will not be put to shame.' Jesus gives riches to all who call on him. For everyone who calls on the name of the Lord will be saved" (Romans 10:9–13).

Romans 12:9–21 gives a great summary of how we are supposed to act as followers of Jesus.

Let love be genuine. Abhor what is evil, hold fast to what is good. Love one another in brotherly affection. Outdo one another in showing honor. Do not be slothful in zeal, be fervent in spirit, serve the Lord. Rejoice in hope, be patient in tribulation, be constant in prayer. Contribute to the needs of the saints and seek to show hospitality.

Bless those who persecute you; bless and do not curse them. Rejoice with those who rejoice, weep with those who weep. Live in harmony with one another. Do not be haughty, but associate with the lowly. Never be wise in your own sight. Repay no one evil for evil, but give thought to do what is honorable in the sight of all. If possible, so far as it depends on you, live peaceably with all. Beloved, never avenge yourselves, but leave it to the wrath of God, for it is written, "Vengeance is mine, I will repay, says the Lord." To the contrary, "if your enemy is hungry, feed him; if he is thirsty, give him something to drink; for by doing so you will heap burning coals on his head." Do not be overcome by evil, but overcome evil with good.

If you love other people, you will do what God wants you to do and keep the commandments (Romans 13:8–10).

"We who are strong have an obligation to bear with the failings of the weak, and not to please ourselves. Let each of us please his neighbor for his good, to build him or her up. For Jesus did not please himself, but as it is written, "The reproaches of those who reproached you fell on me" (Romans 15:1–3).

"The God of peace will soon crush Satan under your feet" (Romans 16:20).

The First Letter of Paul to the Corinthians

God chooses to use people who are weak and may not have many talents to do his work for him. People who are talented or powerful tend to get conceited when God uses them, so he likes to use ordinary people to do great things instead (1 Corinthians 1:26–31).

"What no eyes have seen, nor ear heard, nor the heart of man imagined, what God has prepared for those who love him" (1 Corinthians 2:9).

"Do you not know that you are God's temple and God's spirit lives in you? If anyone destroys God's temple, God will destroy him. For God's temple is holy, and YOU are that temple" (1 Corinthians 3:16–17).

"Do you not know that your body is a temple of the Holy Spirit within you, whom you have from God? You are not your own, for you were bought with a price. So glorify God in your body" (1 Corinthians 6:19–20).

"No temptation has overtaken you that is not common to man. God is faithful, and he will not let you be tempted beyond your ability, but with the temptation he will also provide the way of escape, that you may be able to endure it" (1 Corinthians 10:13).

"Let no one seek his own good, but the good of his neighbor" (1 Corinthians 10:24).

We all have jobs to do as members of the family or body of Jesus. Just as each of our body parts are different and have specific jobs to do, each part is important (1 Corinthians 12:14–31).

Treating each other with love and in a caring manner is by far the most important thing that we can do as followers of Jesus. We should treat everyone with love and care in *everything that we do* (1 Corinthians 13:1–13).

"But in fact Christ has been raised from the dead, the firstfruits of those who have fallen asleep. For as by a man came death (Adam), by a man has come also the resurrection of the dead (Jesus). For as in Adam all die, so also in Christ shall all be made alive" (1 Corinthians 15:20–22).

When we die and go to heaven, we will get a glorious, spectacular spiritual body that will live forever and will be in the image of Jesus (1 Corinthians 15:42–58).

The Second Letter of Paul to the Corinthians

God comforts and helps us so that we are in good shape to comfort and help other people (2 Corinthians 1:3–7).

"We do not lose heart. Though our outer self is wasting away, our inner self is being renewed day by day. For this light momentary affliction is preparing us for an eternal weight of glory beyond all comparison, as we look not to the things that are seen but to the things that are unseen. For the things that are seen are temporary, but the things that are unseen are eternal" (2 Corinthians 4:16–18).

Jesus took all of our sins and placed them on himself when he was crucified, so we will be seen as completely holy and sinless in the eyes of God. We are ambassadors for Jesus to other people in the world. God sends his messages about himself to the rest of the world through his followers. We are the ones who spread his messages to everyone (2 Corinthians 5:16–21).

"Whoever sows sparingly will also reap sparingly, and whoever sows bountifully will also reap bountifully. Each one must give as he decided in his heart, not reluctantly or under compulsion, for God loves a cheerful giver" (2 Corinthians 9:6–7).

"Fourteen years ago I (Paul) was taken up to heaven, taken to paradise. I heard things which cannot be told, which man may not speak of. To keep me from being conceited because of the surpassing greatness of the revelations, a thorn was given me in the flesh, a messanger of Satan to harass me to keep me from becoming conceited. Three times I pleaded with the Lord about this, that it should leave me. But he said to me 'My grace is sufficient for you, for my power is made perfect in weakness.' For the sake of Christ, then, I am content with weakness, insults, hardships, persecutions and calamities. For when I am weak, then I am strong" (2 Corinthians 12:2–10).

"Examine yourselves, to see whether you are in the faith. Test yourselves. Or do you not realize this about yourselves, that Jesus Christ is in you?" (2 Corinthians 13:5).

"Finally brothers, rejoice. Aim for restoration, comfort one another, agree with one another, live in peace: and the God of love and peace will be with you" (2 Corinthians 13:11).

The Book of Galatians

God sent Peter to teach the Jewish people about Jesus, and God sent Paul to teach everyone else about Jesus (Galatians 2:7).

"I have been crucified with Christ. It is no longer I who live, but Christ who lives in me. And the life I now live in the flesh I live by faith in the Son of God, who loved me and gave himself for me" (Galatians 2:20).

"Let us not grow tired of doing good, for in due season we will be rewarded for it, if we do not give up. So then, when we have the opportunity, let us do good to everyone" (Galatians 6:9–10).

The Book of Ephesians

Jesus chose each one of us to be his before he created the world. We are his adopted children through what Jesus did for us. Because Jesus died to pay for our sins, our sins are forgiven. As God's children, we will receive a great inheritance when we get to heaven (Ephesians 1:3–14). For those who accept Jesus, God will show us the immeasurable riches of his kindness toward us when we get to heaven (Ephesians 2:4–7).

Do not let the sun go down on your anger. If you are angry, do not commit sins due to your anger. Give no opportunity to the devil. Let no bad talk come out of your mouths, but only talk that is good for building others up that it may help those who hear it. Do not grieve the Holy Spirit of God, by whom you were sealed for the day of redemption. (Remember, the Holy Spirit lives in you.) Get rid of all your bitterness and anger, hatred, and gossip about others. Be kind to one another, tenderhearted, and forgiving one another, as God in Christ forgave you (Ephesians 4:25–32).

The Book of Philippians

It is great to be alive and well here on earth. But things will be even better when those of us who follow Jesus die, go to heaven, and are with him there (Philippians 1:21–26).

"For it has been granted to you that for the sake of Christ you should not only believe in him but also suffer for his sake, engaged in the same conflict that you saw I had and now hear that I still have" (Philippians 1:29–30). (Paul was writing this letter from prison. He was put in prison for teaching about Jesus.)

Be humble and put other's needs before your own interests, just as Jesus did (Philippians 2:1–11).

The Book of Colossians

Jesus, as God, created everything that exists, and he holds everything together that exists. And although all of us have done bad things in our lives, he saved us by accepting punishment that should have been ours and dying for our sins. If we accept him and what he did for us, we become holy, sinless, and blameless when judged by him when we die (Colossians 1:15–23).

"And you, who were dead in your trespasses (sins), God made alive together with him, having forgiven us all our trespasses, by cancelling the record of debt that stood against us with its legal demands. This he set aside, nailing it to the cross" (Colossians 2:13–14).

Set your mind on God and getting to heaven, not on getting things on earth. One day you will be with Jesus in glory (Colossians 3:1–4). Then Colossians 3:12–17 talks about the daily attitude you should have.

Put on then, as God's chosen ones, holy and beloved, compassionate hearts, kindness, humility, meekness, and patience, bearing with one another and, if one has a complaint against another, forgiving each other; as the Lord has forgiven you, so you must also forgive. And above all these put on love, which binds everything together in perfect harmony. And let the peace of Christ rule in your hearts, to which indeed you were called in one body. And be thankful. Let the word of Christ dwell in you richly, teaching and admonishing one another in all wisdom, singing psalms and hymns and spiritual songs, with thankfulness in your hearts to God. And whatever you do, in word or deed, do everything in the name of the Lord Jesus, giving thanks to God the Father through him.

1 Thessalonians 4:13–18 says that, at some point in the future, Jesus will descend from heaven and appear in the sky. Then he will bring to heaven those who believed in him and died. Next, Jesus will take those that are alive on earth who believe in him straight up to meet him in the air and then to heaven with him while they are alive. This is called the rapture.

God has not destined us for wrath, but to obtain salvation through our Lord Jesus Christ, who died for us so that whether we are awake or asleep we might live with him. Therefore, encourage one another and build one another up, just as you are doing. (1 Thessalonians 5:9–11)

We urge you, brothers, admonish the idle, encourage the fainthearted, help the weak, be patient with them all. See that no one repays anyone evil for evil, but always seek to do good to one another and to everyone. Rejoice always, pray without ceasing, give thanks in all circumstances; for this is the will of God in Christ Jesus for you. (1 Thessalonians 5:14–18)

The Book of 2 Thessalonians

"Those people who do not know God and who do not obey the gospel of our Lord Jesus, God will inflict vengeance and these people will suffer the punishment of eternal destruction, away from the presence of the Lord and from the glory of his might" (2 Thessalonians 1:8–9).

At some point in the future, there will be a rebellion against God on earth. At this time, the Holy Spirit, who is restraining the appearance of the Antichrist, will be removed from the earth. This will likely be the rapture. The Holy Spirit is on earth, living inside those of us that follow Jesus.

For him to be removed, we have to be taken off the earth. Then the Antichrist will appear and deceive many into following and worshipping him as a god through using false signs and wonders. Many of the people that rebelled against God prior to this will follow the Antichrist. At some point, Jesus will return to earth and completely destroy the Antichrist just by speaking words at him (2 Thessalonians 2:1–12).

"Christ Jesus came into the world to save sinners, of whom I am first" (1 Timothy 1:15).

Be godly and content with what you have. As long as we have food and clothing, everything else is extra blessings. People who desire to be rich often fall into temptation and destroy their lives (1 Timothy 6:6–10).

"As for the rich in this present age, they should not be conceited, and they should not set their hopes on the uncertainty of riches, but on God, who richly provides us with everything to enjoy. They are to do good, do a lot of good works, and be generous and ready to share, thus storing up treasure for themselves as a good foundation for the future, so that they may take hold of what is truly life" (1 Timothy 6:17–19).

God did not give us a spirit of fear, but of power, love, and self-control (2 Timothy 1:7).

When we suffer in life, we offer our suffering up to Jesus. This allows us to share in our suffering with him, just as he had suffered for us when he died on the cross. This then allows us to earn the rewards that God has set aside for us because we shared in the suffering of his Son (2 Timothy 2:3–10).

"If we have died with him, we will also live with him; If we endure, we will also reign with him; if we deny him, he also will deny us" (2 Timothy 2:11–12).

"The Lord's servant must not be quarrelsome but kind to everyone, able to teach, patiently enduring evil, correcting his opponents with gentleness" (2 Timothy 2:24–25).

The Book of Titus

"Remind them to be submissive to rulers and authorities, to be obedient, to be ready for every good work, to speak evil of no one, to avoid quarreling, to be gentle, and to show perfect courtesy toward all people" (Titus 3:1–2).

The Book of Hebrews

> Long ago, at many times and in many ways, God spoke to our fathers by the prophets, but in these last days he has spoken to us by his Son, whom he appointed the heir of all things, through whom also he created the world. He is the radiance of the glory of God and the exact imprint of his nature, and he upholds the universe by the word of his power. After making purification for sins, he sat down at the right hand of the Majesty on high, having become as much superior to angels as the name he has inherited is more excellent than theirs. (Hebrews 1:1–4)

Angels are spirits that God sends out to help the people who believe in and follow Jesus. "Are they (angels) not all ministering spirits sent out to serve for the sake of those who are to inherit salvation?" (Hebrews 1:14).

"Do not regard lightly the discipline of the Lord, nor be weary when reproved by him. For the Lord disciplines the one he loves, and chastises every son whom he receives" (Hebrews 12:5–6).

God disciplines us so that we turn out good because he is our father and we are his children (Hebrews 12:7–11).

"Strive for peace with everyone, and for the holiness without which no one will see the Lord" (Hebrews 12:14).

"Do not neglect to show hospitality to strangers, for thereby some have entertained angels unawares" (Hebrews 13:2).

"Keep your life free from the love of money, and be content with what you have, for God has said 'I will never leave you nor forsake you.' So we can confidently say, 'The Lord is my helper; I will not fear; what can man do to me?'" (Hebrews 13:5–6).

"Do not neglect to do good and share what you have, for such sacrifices are pleasing to God" (Hebrews 13:16).

The Book of James

"Count it all joy, my brothers, when you meet trials of various kinds, for you know that the testing of your faith produces steadfastness. And let steadfastness have its full effect, that you may be perfect and complete, lacking in nothing" (James 1:2–4).

"Let no one say when he is tempted, 'I am being tempted by God,' for God cannot be tempted with evil, and he himself tempts no one. But each person is tempted when he is lured and enticed by his own desire. Then desire when it has conceived gives birth to sin, and sin when it is fully grown brings forth death" (James 1:13–15).

"Do not be deceived, my beloved brothers. Every good gift and every perfect gift is from above, coming down from the Father of lights with whom there is no variation or shadow due to change" (James 1:16–17).

"Let every person be quick to hear, slow to speak, slow to anger; for the anger of man does not produce the righteousness of God" (James 1:19–20).

"Be doers of the Word of God, and not hearers only, deceiving yourselves. Religion that is pure and undefiled before God, the Father, is this: to visit orphans and widows in their affliction, and to keep oneself unstained form the world" (James 1:22, 27).

Do not treat people differently if they are rich or poor or popular or unpopular. Treat everyone well (James 2–7).

"What good is it, my brothers, if someone says he has faith but does not have works? Can that faith save him? If a brother or a sister is poorly clothed and lacking in daily food, and one of you says to them, 'Go in peace, be warm and filled,' without giving them the things needed for the body, what good is that? So also faith by itself, if it does not have works, is dead" (James 2:14–17).

"Submit yourselves to God. Resist the devil and he will flee from you. Draw near to God and he will draw near to you" (James 4:7–8).

"Whoever knows the right thing to do and fails to do it, for him it is sin" (James 4:17).

"If anyone among you wanders from the truth and someone brings him back, let him know that whoever brings back a sinner from his wandering will save his soul from death and will cover a multitude of sins" (James 5:19–20).

The First Letter of Peter

"Blessed be the God and Father of our Lord Jesus Christ! According to his great mercy, he has caused us to be born again to a living hope through the resurrection of Jesus Christ from the dead, to an inheritance that is imperishable, undefiled, and unfading, kept in heaven for you, who by God's power are being guarded through faith for a salvation ready to be revealed in the last time. Though you do not now see Jesus, you believe in him and rejoice with joy that is inexpressible and filled with glory, obtaining the outcome of your faith, the salvation of your souls" (1 Peter 1:3–5, 8–9).

"Jesus bore our sins in his body on the tree that we might die to sin and live to righteousness. By his wounds you have been healed. For you were straying like sheep, but now have returned to the Shepherd and Overseer of your souls" (1 Peter 2:24–25).

"Finally, all of you, have unity of mind, sympathy, brotherly love, a tender heart, and a humble mind. Do not repay evil for evil or reviling for reviling, but on the contrary, bless, for to this you were called, that you may obtain a blessing. For 'Whoever desires to love life and see good days, let him keep his tongue from evil and his lips from speaking deceit; let him turn away from evil and do good; let him seek peace and pursue it. For the eyes of the Lord are on the righteous, and his ears are open to their prayer. But the face of the Lord is against those who do evil'" (1 Peter 3:8–12).

"Above all, keep loving one another earnestly, since love covers a multitude of sins. Show hospitality to one another without grumbling" (1 Peter 4:8–10).

"Beloved, do not be surprised at the fiery trial when it comes upon you to test you, as though something strange were happening to you. But rejoice insofar as you share Christ's sufferings, that you may also rejoice and be glad when his glory is revealed. If you are insulted for the name of Christ, you are blessed, because the Spirit of glory and of God rests upon you" (1 Peter 12–14).

"Humble yourselves, therefore, under the mighty hand of God so that at the proper time he may exalt you, casting all your anxieties on him, because he cares for you. Be sober minded; be watchful. Your adversary the devil prowls around like a roaring lion, seeking someone to devour. Resist him, firm in your faith, knowing that the same kinds of suffering are being experienced by your brotherhood throughout the world. And after you have suffered a little while, the God of all grace, who has called you to his eternal glory in Christ, will himself restore, confirm, strengthen, and establish you. To him be the dominion forever and ever. Amen" (1 Peter 5:6–11).

The Second Letter of Peter

"No prophesy of Scripture comes from someone's own interpretation. For no prophesy was ever produced by the will of man, but men spoke from God as they were carried along by the Holy Spirit" (2 Peter 1:20–21).

"The Lord is not slow to fulfill his promise as some count slowness, but is patient toward you, not wishing that any should perish, but that all should reach repentance" (2 Peter 3:9).

The First Letter of John

If anyone does sin, we have an advocate with the Father, Jesus Christ the righteous. He is the propitiation for our sins, and not for ours only but also for the sins of the whole world. And by this we know that we have come to know him, if we keep his commandments. Whoever says "I know him" but does not keep his commandments is a liar, and the truth is not in him, but whoever keeps his word, in him truly the love of God is perfected. By this we may know that we are in him: whoever says he abides in him ought to walk in the same way in which he walked" (1 John 2:1–6).

"Do not love the world or the things in the world. If anyone loves the world, the love of the Father is not in him. For all that is in the world—the desires of the flesh and the desires of the eyes and pride in possessions—is not from the Father but is from the world. And the world is passing away along with its desires, but whoever does the will of God abides forever" (1 John 2:15–17).

"By this we know love, that he (Jesus) laid down his life for us, and we ought to lay down our lives for the brothers. But if anyone has the world's goods and sees his brother in need, yet closes his heart against him, how does God's love abide in him? Little children, let us not love in word or talk but in deed and truth" (1 John 3:16–19).

"God's commandment to us is that we believe in the name of His Son Jesus Christ and that we love one another" (1 John 3:23).

"Beloved, let us love one another, for love is from God, and whoever loves has been born of God and knows God. Anyone who does not love does not know God, because God is love. In this the love of God was made manifest among us, that God sent his only Son into the world, so that we might live through him. In this is love, not that we have loved God but that he loved us and sent his Son to be the propitiation for our sins. Beloved, if God so loved us, we also ought to love one another. No one has ever seen God; if we love one another, God abides in us and his love is perfected in us" (1 John 4:7–12).

"Whoever confesses that Jesus is the Son of God, God abides in him, and he in God" (1 John 4:15).

"If anyone says 'I love God', and hates his brother, he is a liar; for he who does not love his brother who he has seen cannot love God whom he has not seen. And this commandment we have from him: whoever loves God must also love his brother" (1 John 4:20–21).

"God gave us eternal life, and this life is in his Son. Whoever has the Son has life; whoever does not have the Son of God does not have life" (1 John 5:11–12).

"This is the confidence that we have toward God, that if we ask anything **according to his will** he hears us. And if we know that he hears us in whatever we ask, we know that we have the requests that we ask of him" (1 John 5:14–15).

"We know that everyone who has been born of God does not keep on sinning, but he who was born of God protects him, and the evil one does not touch him" (1 John 8:18).

The Third Letter of John

"Do not imitate evil but imitate good. Whoever does good is from God; whoever does evil has not seen God" (3 John 1:11).

The Letter of Jude

Read Jude 1:5–6. It talks about how Jesus, when he was up in heaven as God, punished the Egyptians for mistreating the Israelites and the angels who rebelled against God.

Chapter 22

The Book of Revelation

This chapter is a combination of the Book of Revelation, and the prophetic books of the old testament about the end times. The book of Revelation is about the future. It tells about the events around the time when Jesus will come back to earth. The apostle John, Jesus's best friend, wrote it. John was the only apostle to die of old age. All of the other apostles were martyred (killed) because government leaders told them repeatedly to stop teaching about Jesus, but they would not cease. So the Jewish religious leaders killed all of the other apostles.

Although John was not killed, he wrote the book of Revelation while stranded as a prisoner on the island of Patmos, where they sent prisoners to live. God sent an angel to the apostle John while he was on the island of Patmos. He showed John things that would happen in the world around the time of Jesus's return, and John was instructed to write this down.

The Holy Spirit was also guiding John on what to write. Additionally the resurrected Jesus appeared to John and showed and told him what to write. We do not know when these future events will take place. It could be during our lifetime or a long way in the future.

During the time on earth recorded in the book of Revelation, the world will be going through the worst series of events ever. God says that never before did the world go through such terrible things, and it will never again go through them after. The good news is that those who are alive during the period of Revelation and love Jesus will miss all of these bad things.

The Bible says there will be something called a rapture. Jesus will come and take all of the people who love and follow him up into the air to meet him in the sky while they are alive. They will go to heaven to be with him while they are alive and miss all of these bad things concerning the Antichrist.

That is because we love him and we do not deserve to go through the harsh punishment of the earth. That is for people who do not love him. It is to let them see in person who God and the devil is and to allow them to make a choice of who they will follow. Since we already follow God, we are saved from going through all of these bad things. It is a forced choice for the remaining people on earth who do not yet follow Jesus: choose now either to follow him or to not follow him and follow the devil instead.

The time for this first period of humanity between Adam to the people in the time of Revelation is up. God wants to move to the next period of humanity, a thousand-year span in which Jesus is on earth, governing the entire world in person. For that to happen, this present period must end, and everyone alive must make a choice of whom he or she will follow, Jesus or the devil. Those who already follow Jesus made their choice and are saved by the rapture while alive during the Revelation. For the rest left behind, the seven-year period during the Revelation is where they *have to make a choice*.

Right before these events take place and Jesus returns, things will be very bad in the world. There will be many natural disasters such as earthquakes, hurricanes, and volcano eruptions. Things will happen that will poison some of the water on the earth, making it undrinkable. There will be wars going on in many parts of the world.

During this time, God will send two witnesses to Jerusalem. Many Bible scholars believe that these two witnesses are Moses and Elijah. These two witnesses will stand in Jerusalem and preach or tell people about God for three and a half years. God will give them special powers. If anyone tries to hurt them, fire will come out of their mouths at the people who are trying to hurt them. God will give them power to stop the rain from falling, to turn rivers and lakes into blood, and to cause any type of plague to fall on the people as often as they want. The whole world will see these two witnesses preaching on television, the internet, or whatever other communication devices will be used at this future date, and they will hear their message that we must all follow and trust in Jesus to be saved.

Also during this time, the devil will possess and give power to two world leaders. The first one will be called the Antichrist. He will be a political and/or military leader. He will manipulate his way into power by lies and flattery. Because the devil gives him power, he will seem smarter and more powerful than everybody else. Many people on the earth will accept him as a world ruler because they believe he is the only one smart enough to fix all of the world's severe problems at that time.

The second world leader that the devil will give power to will be called the false prophet. He will be a religious leader. The devil will give him power to do great miracles that will amaze the people of the world, such as making fire come down from the sky for everyone to see. He also lies to everyone, telling the world that they need to follow and worship the Antichrist because he is a good leader. (He is really empowered by the devil.)

God says many times that, when these things happen in the world, do not be afraid. God is always in control of everything. He will allow these things to happen so that people can have the free will to choose whom they will follow, God or the devil. We must always follow God no matter what difficult things happen down here on earth.

When the Antichrist first comes to power as a world leader, he will be granted seven years to rule on the earth. In the beginning, he will seem like the smartest guy in the world who will fix the world's problems. Halfway through his rule (three and a half years), he will enter the temple in Jerusalem with TV cameras from all over the world on him. He will sit on the throne in the temple and say that, not only is he the ruler of the world, he is also God and everyone must worship him or he or she will be punished.

He will make everyone take a mark of his number, 666, on his or her right hand or forehead. People will not be able to buy or sell anything without this mark. God says that whoever is on earth at the time must not take the mark because, if they do, they are following the devil and will be condemned. God promises to take care of us who love him and do not take the mark.

While the Antichrist is on earth, God will send three angels to fly around the world, continually preaching messages from God to the people on the earth. The first angel will preach the gospel to the world so everyone has a chance to hear about Jesus and choose to follow him to be saved if he or she wants to.

The second angel will tell the world that the great evil that is taking place in the world is about to be destroyed. The third angel will tell the world that whoever worships the Antichrist and takes the mark of the beast (666) on his or her hand or forehead will go to hell when he or she dies.

God says that whoever worships God/Jesus during these times will go to heaven when they die.

During this time, there will be wars and chaos all over the world. There will be several groups of countries fighting each other. The Antichrist will be the ruler of the most powerful army at that time, but there will be other groups of countries and armies fighting against him and with each other.

At one point, all of the armies on earth will gather for the biggest battle in the history of the world. This battle will take place on a large plain in Israel called Megiddo. It will be called the Battle of Armageddon. Two hundred million soldiers from different forces will show up to fight this battle. The Antichrist and his armies will be there to fight.

Just as all of these armies are about to fight each other in the Battle of Armageddon, Jesus will return to earth! When he ascended to heaven in front of the apostles after he was resurrected from being dead for three days when he was crucified, he rose up to heaven on the Mount of Olives in Jerusalem. The angels told the apostles at the time that someday Jesus will return a second time on the Mount of Olives. This is what happens.

Jesus will descend from heaven and land on the Mount of Olives, and the whole world will witness this. He will have so much power when he returns that, where he lands on the Mount of Olives, the mountain will split into two. It will create a wide valley because half of the Mount of Olives will move northward and the other half will move southward.

"On that day there will be no light, cold, or frost. And there shall be a unique day, which is known to the Lord, neither day nor night, but at evening there shall be light" (Zechariah 14:1–7).

Jesus climbs on a white horse from heaven to fight the Antichrist and the 200 million-man armies.

> His eyes are like a flame of fire, and on his head are many diadems, and he has a name written that no one knows but himself. He is clothed in a robe dipped in blood, and the name by which he is called is The Word of God. And the armies of heaven, arrayed in fine linen, white and pure, were following him on white horses. From his mouth comes a sharp sword with which to strike down the nations, and he will rule them with a rod of iron. On his robe and on his thigh he has a name written, "King of kings and Lord of lords." (Revelation 19:11–16)

When the Antichrist and the armies of the earth see Jesus coming with the armies of heaven, they will try to fight against Jesus. Jesus will capture the Antichrist and the false prophet, who deceived the people who had received the mark of the beast, or Antichrist (666). The antichrist and false prophet will be thrown alive into the lake of fire in hell. Jesus will then kill all of the evil soldiers who were in the 200 million-man armies by the sword that comes out of Jesus's mouth. (Jesus just spoke something, and all of the bad soldiers fell over dead.)

Next, an angel will come down from heaven, holding in his hand the key to the bottomless pit and a great chain. He will grab the devil, or Satan, and chain him up for a thousand years in the bottomless pit. He will seal it over him so he might not deceive the nations any longer until the thousand years are ended. After that, Satan will be released for a little while.

Jesus will set up his throne in Jerusalem, and he will rule everyone on earth from there for a thousand years. Since Satan will be chained up for a thousand years, he will not be roaming around, causing problems anymore. Also, since Jesus is running everything in person, everything will be great! There will be no more wars or major problems in the world. Jesus will govern the world, and his government will be perfect.

While Jesus is ruling in person on earth, even the animals will be at peace. They will no longer eat each other. They will all become plant eaters. Animals will never be dangerous to people again.

> The wolf shall dwell with the lamb, and the leopard shall lie down with the young goat, and the calf and the lion and the fattened calf together; and a little child shall lead them. The cows and the bear shall graze; their young shall lie down together; and the lion shall eat straw like the ox. The nursing child shall play over the hole of the cobra, and the weaned child shall put his hand on the adder's (snake's) den. They shall not hurt or destroy in all my holy mountain; for the earth shall be full of the knowledge of the Lord as the waters cover the sea. (Isaiah 11:6–9)

People will return to Jerusalem to live where Jesus will govern the world from. There will be great happiness with children playing in the streets, and people will live to be hundreds of years old. A person who is a hundred years old will be considered a young man or woman (Zechariah 8:1–8; Isaiah 65:17–25).

People will come from all over the world to Jerusalem to talk with and worship Jesus. Leaders of countries from all around the world will come to seek counsel and advice from him. The city of Jerusalem will be called the throne of the Lord. There will be no more wars at all in the world under the rule of Jesus (Isaiah 2:1–5). Jesus will make Jerusalem a glorious place, and the whole world will come to visit him there (Isaiah 60:1–22).

Christians who believe in Jesus will be raptured and miss all of the bad things that will happen on earth while the Antichrist is running loose. After the followers of Jesus have been raptured, of those who were left behind, there will be many people who will come to Jesus and follow him during this time on earth. They will reject the Antichrist and refuse to follow him. The Antichrist will kill many of them for following Jesus and not him. These people who died for following Jesus during the Revelation period will be brought back to life and will return with Jesus to earth when he comes back. They will reign on earth with Jesus during this thousand-year period (Revelation 20:1–6).

At the end of this thousand-year period of Jesus's reign on earth, Satan will be released from being chained up in the bottomless pit. This is to give the people on earth a choice again of whom they want to follow: God or the devil. Satan will once again deceive the nations of the world and gather them for battle. He will have armies from parts of the world surround the city of Jerusalem where Jesus will be living.

Once they surround the city to attack Jesus and his followers, however, God will send fire down from the sky, which will consume all of these evil armies. Jesus will then throw the devil into hell, and he will never be let out to bother anyone again.

Next is what is called the great white throne judgment. Everyone who ever died will stand before God and be judged on whether he or she loved and followed Jesus or not after hearing about him. Those who did choose to love and follow God will have their names written in the Lamb's Book of Life and will be allowed to enter and live in heaven forever.

God will make a new heaven and a new earth, and he will live with us there. God will make a New Jerusalem and send it down to the new earth from the new heaven. There will be no sun, moon, or lights in the city. Light will come out of the glory of God and light the city up. It will always be day there. There will never be night or darkness in New Jerusalem. Everyone around the world will be welcome to come there, and its city gates will never be shut. God himself will come and live with the people as their God.

> There will be the river of the water of life flowing from the throne of God and the Lamb through the middle street of Jerusalem. On either side of the river of life will be the tree of life. Its leaves will heal the nations. No longer will there be anything accursed. **(The curse put on mankind when Adam and Eve sinned will finally be removed).** The Throne of God and the Lamb will be in the world, and his servants will see his face and his name will be on their foreheads. And night will be no more. They will need no light or lamp or sun, for the Lord God will be their light, and they will reign forever and ever. (Revelation 22:1–5)

Jesus ends the Bible by saying,

> Behold, I am coming soon, bringing my payment with me, to repay everyone for what he has done. I am the Alpha and the Omega, the first and the last, the beginning and the end. I, Jesus, have sent my angel to testify to you about these things for the churches. I am the root and descendant of David, the bright morning star. Surely I am coming soon. (Revelation 22:12–20)

About the Author

I am a licensed psychologist in the state of Pennsylvania. I have been practicing at a Christian counseling private practice since 2006, and I have experience in a variety of counseling and human services positions since 1989.

I have under contract to have four Christian books published this year:

- *Faith Through Your Hardships Draws Others to Christ* (Westbow Press)
- *Lessons for Christians from the Trials of Job* (Christian Faith Publishing)
- *The Good Things Jesus Does for Us, to Us, and Through Us* (Christian Faith Publishing)
- *Temptations and Trials Faced by Bible Legends* (Westbow Press) (November 2018)

Printed in the USA
CPSIA information can be obtained
at www.ICGtesting.com
LVHW040035230923
758639LV00001B/1